CAMBODIA

Michael Leifer

CAMBODIA

THE SEARCH FOR SECURITY

FREDERICK A. PRAEGER, *Publishers*
New York · Washington · London

FREDERICK A. PRAEGER, PUBLISHERS
111 Fourth Avenue, New York, N.Y. 10003, U.S.A.
77–79 Charlotte Street, London W.1, England

Published in the United States of America in 1967
by Frederick A. Praeger, Inc., Publishers

Printed in the United States of America

For
FRANCES

Acknowledgments

My interest in Cambodia was stimulated by a sojourn of more than three years in Australia, a country whose citizens are exhorted continually to look to their "near north." I fell prey to this growing national habit. This interest was sustained when I returned to England to the Centre for South East Asian Studies in the University of Hull.

I should like to thank George Modelski, who was responsible for extending an invitation to a visiting fellowship at the Australian National University and so made possible my initial venture into the realm of Cambodian foreign policy. At the University of Adelaide, Professor W. G. K. Duncan was kind enough to look with benevolence on my exotic interests. I should like to express my appreciation to the members of the Board of South East Asian Studies of the University of Hull for making available the finance for visits to Cambodia and other parts of Southeast Asia. I am also indebted to Willard Hanna, whose initiative was in part responsible for my attempting this study. Finally, I should like to thank Miss V. Howlett for typing the bulk of the manuscript, my wife for helping in its completion, and the staff of Frederick A. Praeger, Inc., for invaluable editorial assistance.

Any errors of fact or interpretation are my own.

MICHAEL LEIFER

Hull
March, 1967

vii

Contents

CAMBODIA

1

Introducing Cambodia

To the visitor, the Kingdom of Cambodia presents an attractive aspect. From the air, there are glimpses of the confluence of waterways at Phnom Penh; on land, there are impressive educational showpieces along the highway from the airport and then the neat capital of Phnom Penh itself, whose French provincial charm has been embellished by local efforts of beautification. Lush ricelands, haunting forested ranges, coastal and hill resorts, and, of course, the majestic splendors of Angkor add to the country's attraction. Signs of economic development blend with scenes of traditional character in a picture of the happy coexistence of modern and past modes. This is the visage of Cambodia that the visitor often sees; it is certainly the face that is continually presented to the outside world by a zealous Ministry of Information.

This book, however, is not concerned with the picturesque. Its purpose is to focus on the problems of external security that Cambodia has faced since independence and, where relevant, to consider the domestic political background of that self-styled "peaceful oasis in the inferno of Southeast Asia." I shall attempt to sketch briefly the salient features of contemporary Cambodia as a preliminary to the chief objective of this study.

3

Land and People

Situated in the southern portion of the Indochinese Peninsula, with a coastline on the Gulf of Siam, Cambodia has common boundaries with Thailand, Laos, and South Viet-Nam. Cambodia is shaped like a distorted circle and is about 67,000 square miles in size—approximately the combined area of England and Wales. Most of the country is a flat plain, but on the periphery there are high plateaus and mountain ranges—the Dangreks in the northwest, and the Cardamomes in the southwest. There is also hilly-to-mountainous country in the north and east, along the frontier with Laos and South Viet-Nam. Through the lowland area run two major waterways, the Mekong and the Tonlé Sap. The Mekong flows southward through Laos and into the delta country of South Viet-Nam. The Tonlé Sap rises in the northwest and takes the form of a great lake of changing dimensions some distance upstream from Phnom Penh. The two rivers converge at Phnom Penh, whose location makes it a major port.

Cambodia's climate is hot and humid, with a rainy season from May to November. Although the lowland soil is not remarkably fertile and in many places restricts yield, periodic flooding by the Mekong and the Tonlé Sap makes possible a wet-rice agriculture that supplies a moderate surplus for export. Self-sufficiency in rice, an abundance of fish, and a limited production of vegetables provide an ample subsistence diet for the largely rural population of approximately 6 million. There is little poverty by Asian standards, and certainly nothing to compare with the pitiful state .of many of India's millions. In general, there is moderate peasant indebtedness and no acute land shortage. Landholding tends to be on an individual basis, although the government is seeking to sponsor cooperative ventures in the interests of higher production. Approximately 80 per cent of the cultivable land is devoted to rice; its production is the chief occupation of the people as well as the principal export. Not surprisingly, the major areas of population settlement are those nourished by the great waterways.

The Khmers, who constitute the dominant ethnic group (over 5 million), trace their ancestry and traditions to the Kambuja period. Khmer minorities also live across the Thai and South Vietnamese borders. The Khmers probably originated in the southwestern provinces of China, but the chief influences that have shaped their culture are Indian. These influences were well established in the pre-Angkor kingdoms of Funan and Chen-la, and vestiges of ancient practices are found in court offices and rituals. Cultural blending is as much a fact of Cambodian life as racial mixing. The result of the latter is the present-day Khmer. The language of the indigenous majority is also known as Khmer, and in terms of linguistic classification it is included in the Mon-Khmer category, which is related to the Munda languages of western Bengal.

In their rural environment, the Khmers are conservative villagers who live mainly in simple thatched houses raised on wooden piles. Kinship ties are of a very flexible patrilineal and matrilineal kind, and family extension and affiliation are essentially a function of living recollection rather than village records.[1] Although the limited but rapidly growing urban centers demonstrate the influence of the modern world, the vast majority of the population has not yet been deeply affected by the process of modernization. The transistorized radio and the bicycle are perhaps the most common signs of changing rural modes. The rhythm of life is still governed by the cultivation of rice, which is accomplished chiefly by traditional methods and accompanied by appropriate religious ritual.

Religion is a dominant factor in rural life, and Buddhist ethics mingle with the long-established folk religion that reveres the spirits believed to reside in physical objects. Theravada Buddhism is the formal religion of the majority of the people, and the government takes great care not to offend the sensibilities of the Buddhist monks, who are very close to the rural dwellers. The head of state, Prince Norodom Sihanouk, goes out of his way to pay respect to the Buddhist hierarchy. He also encourages and participates in traditional ceremonies that have religious connotations. The Buddhist monks represent a potential, if mild, challenge to secular leadership, but at present the religious orders appear content with their role in society.

Government influence is steadily spreading to the villages through increased school building, the establishment of public health facilities, and attempts at community development. At the same time, there is a drift of young men to the urban areas, particularly to the capital, which, in the twenty years after 1945, mushroomed from a town of 50,000 to a city of approximately 500,000. Urban migration is in part a direct result of government activity in the provinces: A taste of education beyond the facilities of the pagoda school often leaves a young man discontented with the life of his parents. Generous expenditure on education (20 per cent of the annual budget), particularly at the secondary level, has intensified the inclination of a good number of Cambodia's youthful generation to move out of agricultural pursuits and to seek employment in occupations that carry greater status and financial reward. Unfortunately, most secondary education in Cambodia is not yet an adequate preparation for the modern world, and there is no immediate prospect that the country will be able to absorb the 15,000 or so young diploma-holders who leave schools each year with little hope of finding satisfying employment. The government seems helpless in the face of a problem it is partly responsible for creating. Indeed, the government is currently engaged in trying to cut public expenditure and reduce the bureaucracy, which has in the past provided the major opening for urban jobless. Youthful unemployed are a potential source of serious political discontent which, if urban living standards continue to deteriorate, could eventually find a national focus for expression.

Economic Development

Cambodia's economy is essentially agricultural, and its chief exports are primary products, with rice, rubber, maize, and pepper accounting for 92 per cent of the total. The nation has made only limited strides in developing an industrial sector and in diversifying an economy whose strength lies in traditional pursuits. In 1953, when Cambodia became independent, the only industrial concerns of consequence were a number of latex plants operated by French-controlled rubber companies, together with a few factories that processed agricultural and forest products. Today, although Cambodia boasts many major industrial enterprises, informed observers express increasing doubt as to the quality of its industrial development.

Cambodia's economic policy has been to achieve a moderate measure of industrialization in some areas to meet an increasing portion of local demand and to save foreign exchange by reducing dependence on imports. Such commendable plans have not been as commendably fulfilled. Industrial development was promoted in the mid-1950's through foreign economic assistance. In June, 1956, the Chinese People's Republic granted Cambodia equipment, construction material, and merchandise allegedly valued at $22.4 million. This assistance was used to build a textile plant, a plywood factory, a cement factory, and a paper mill. These industrial concerns have not been unqualified successes; indeed, in some cases it would seem fair to judge them outright failures. Miscalculations about the proportion of domestic demand in relation to total optimum output and the competitiveness of the product in export markets have led to inefficient operation. Part of the blame lies with the Chinese for supplying machinery of archaic and unsuitable design and part with the Cambodians for building the plants in bad locations, using inferior materials, and providing incompetent and corrupt administration. The plywood factory has been the least rewarding enterprise; the textile plant offers some promise. A similar story can be told about economic assistance from Czechoslovakia for a tractor and automobile plant. While there is an increasing number of vehicles on the streets of Phnom Penh, locally assembled models are conspicuously absent. Better performance is expected of a recently opened sugar refinery, also sponsored by Czechoslovakia, which will use locally produced palm sugar.

Foreign assistance has been more fruitful when used to establish infrastructure for the economy. The principal airport at Poch-entong was developed with French assistance, as was the key port of Sihanoukville on the Gulf of Siam. The port is intended to re-duce dependence on trade on the Mekong River, whose outlet to the sea is controlled by South Viet-Nam. A highway linking the port with the capital was an American benefaction, and a railway line parallel to the highway is now being constructed by the Cam-bodians themselves. Foreign economic aid is continuing on a mod-erate basis; dams for hydroelectric power, for example, have been financed by the Soviet Union, France, and Yugoslavia.

In many ways, the end of 1963 marked a watershed in Cam-bodian economic life. In November, all American economic and military assistance was terminated at the insistence of the Cam-bodian Government. At the same time, the state took over all banks and import-export firms. American aid, which had helped to finance and equip the Cambodian armed services, totaled more than $350 million in the period 1955–62. This represented the great bulk of foreign economic assistance and had contributed in large part to improvements in public health, agricultural development, and educational progress. The initial impact of this rejection of further assistance was softened by good harvests, French credits, and borrowing from the Central Bank. Now, however, Cam-bodia faces serious financial difficulties, which can be traced to excessive government expenditure and the termination of Amer-ican aid. This aid, particularly in the form of budgetary support, allowed a level of expenditure well beyond the earned income of the country. The seriousness of the problem was disguised by a favorable trade balance in 1964, but a poor harvest in 1965 re-vealed the true state of economic affairs and necessitated financial stringency on the part of the government. The urban elite—ac-customed to a high standard of living sustained by American aid —is now finding it difficult to adjust to economic austerity.

Government intervention in the economy has tended to aggra-vate the situation. When the government called for an end to American aid, it also took over banking and foreign trade. This policy succeeded in freezing Chinese business interests in Cambodia, which was the government's intention, but it has had the unfortunate additional effect of inhibiting trade. The government has discovered that its own import-export firms, whose staffs tend to be inflated, are less efficient in commercial enterprise than the Chinese and encourage excessive corruption through a system of licenses similar to the Indonesian practice. With the absence of American aid, the country is less able to afford excesses of corruption on the part of its functionaries and politicians. In May, 1966, Prince Norodom Sihanouk publicly admitted the existence of a crisis in the economy and corruption in public life. He called on the people to inform on profiteers and spoke of the need to cleanse Cambodia's "Augean stables." [2]

The rural sector is not affected in the same way by the financial crisis. Government intervention in agriculture has had mixed reception. Some progress has been made in extending mechanization and improving seed strains, but no fundamental transformation of the rural sector has occurred. There were, for example, only 600 tractors in Cambodia in 1964. In principle, government intervention is designed to make the peasant community less vulnerable to Chinese middlemen, who have had a corner on the market, but the government's rice-purchasing policy has caused some resentment. In practice, it appears that the price offered for rice by government agencies compares unfavorably to that offered by the Chinese, who can find markets across the South Vietnamese frontier. The government is thus meeting increasing rural resistance to implementation of its agricultural policy. This could be serious, because, in the foreseeable future, foreign exchange and the substance of the country's wealth will come almost entirely from agricultural products.

The Cambodian Government makes a great play of its doctrine of Khmer Socialism, which is portrayed as an indigenous ideology designed to promote economic growth. One aspect of this policy is the government's attempt to involve the people in voluntary manual labor. Minor construction works are often accomplished in this way. It is doubtful that this is the most suitable or efficient manner to build a new road or dam, but Sihanouk and his ministers are frequently involved in such enterprises, and the net effect of the policy is to strengthen the ties between rulers and ruled.

Khmer Socialism has its physical status symbols, including a fine national monument, a conference chamber, and an olympic-style stadium, which, in November, 1966, was the site of the First Asian Games of the New Emerging Forces. Although all this is intended to demonstrate that the country's reputation rests on more than historical achievement, if one is to be honest, Khmer Socialism—with its two state-operated shops, selling expensive groceries and inferior, Cambodian-made consumer goods, its mismanagement of the economy, and the opportunities it has provided for corruption—hardly compares with the Oriental despotism that produced the temples of Angkor.

Cambodia's Minorities

As in other parts of Southeast Asia, the growth of communities of ethnic minorities has been a legacy of the colonial era. In Phnom Penh, minorities make up approximately two-thirds of the population. The most significant minority groups are the Vietnamese and the Chinese. The Cham-Malays, who constitute another minority, are descendants in part of the kingdom that collapsed under Vietnamese onslaught in the fifteenth century. Muslim by religion and loyal to the regime by disposition, they are numerically insignificant and politically almost irrelevant. Perhaps more significant in terms of their possible role in a situation of insurgency are the Khmer Loeu, the remnants of the earliest migrations to Cambodia. Displaced from the lowland areas by the ancestors of the contemporary Khmers, the Khmer Loeu now live in the mountainous regions along Cambodia's borders with Laos and Thailand and subsist by traditional slash-and-burn agriculture.

The Vietnamese, who number about 300,000, were assisted in entering Cambodia by the French, who introduced them as estate workers and minor civil servants, but they soon developed other talents as artisans, merchants, and professional people. There is some irony in their presence, in that the French forestalled what had been a gradual Vietnamese expansion at the expense of Cambodian territory only to invite settlement on a lesser scale. The Vietnamese have not been assimilated to any degree and are regarded with considerable suspicion and mistrust. They are believed to have supported the Viet-Minh in Cambodia and also the rebel nationalist Son Ngoc Thanh because of his part-Vietnamese parentage. They are primarily urban dwellers and play no role in national political life, but members of the community are known to have been associated with the pro-Communist Pracheachon (People's) Party, whose masters Sihanouk regards as living in Hanoi. It is claimed also that Vietnamese Communists have infiltrated the Vietnamese community association (the Viet-Kieu) as well as the Vietnamese newspapers and schools in Cambodia. The government has, in the past, sought to exclude the Vietnamese from a number of occupations, but discrimination has been moderate, possibly because of the hostage Cambodian community living in South Viet-Nam.

The Chinese, who also number around 300,000, display talents in economic life similar to those of the Vietnamese. They are more highly regarded than the Vietnamese, however, if only because of the Cambodians' intense dislike of the Vietnamese. Diligence and industry, qualities also found in the Vietnamese, seem to be admired in the Chinese. Cambodians regard the Chinese as desirable sons-in-law. The Chinese have thus been assimilated to a greater degree than the Vietnamese, although they are still identifiable as a separate community, or rather as a collection of separate communities identified by dialect of origin. An absence of Chinese physical intervention in the past may explain the Cambodians' more benevolent attitude toward them. They are not involved in national politics and tend to appear only to cheer a visiting Chinese dignitary or to greet the Chinese ambassador on his way to and from the airport. They were stimulated by the initial contacts with Peking. On Chou En-lai's first visit to Cambodia in November, 1956, a foreign traveler in the country commented: "The Chinese emigrants, most of whom lived in Phnom Penh, laid on such a tremendous welcome that the Khmers almost began to wonder whose country Cambodia was." [3] On the whole, the behavior of the Chinese has been impeccable, although Communist influence exists in several Chinese community organizations and schools.

The Cambodian Government appears concerned mainly about the degree of control that the Chinese and the Vietnamese have been able to exercise over the economy. The nationalization measures of November, 1963, were an attempt to redress the balance of local Khmer control in Cambodia's commercial life.

Politics and Government

Politics occupies the energies of a very small minority of the Cambodian populace. In the main, it is the preserve of a French-speaking elite, whose membership ranges from the royal family to radical schoolteachers. Membership in the dominating mass movement, Sangkum Reastre Niyum (Popular Socialist Community), encompasses, at the periphery, those without family wealth or educational accomplishments, but they are not much involved in the organization's activities.

At the apex of the political structure is the man who was formerly king and who now, as head of state, personifies Cambodia. Prince Norodom Sihanouk enjoys a unique position in terms of both his magnetic appeal to the rural population and the degree to which he controls government action. There is hardly any achievement of the regime for which he does not receive credit. His virtually unchallenged position owes much to his former status as king, a position from which he abdicated in March, 1955. Norodom Sihanouk became king in 1941, when the French by-passed the direct royal line in the hope of placing on the throne a compliant monarch. Sihanouk's father, Norodom Suramarit, a prince of another line, was uninvolved in politics, but, following his son's abdication, accepted the vacant throne to fulfill a ceremonial role. To the peasants, in particular, Prince Sihanouk is semi-divine. One must add to this continuing aura of majesty the reputation he achieved in the campaign to obtain his country's independence and in his continual identification with the interests of his country's security. He is no distant potentate content to remain in a royal palace, but a man who maintains constant contact with the people, whether through public meetings in the capital or extensive travel in the provinces. His practice of holding popular audiences is another way in which he bridges the gap between modern leadership and a traditional people.

There has been no reigning monarch since the death of Sihanouk's father in April, 1960, but the symbolic significance of the throne as a support for the authority of the regime has been sustained. The throne is an appendage to the government and not its rival. In the words of a Ministry of Information publication, "Her Majesty Queen Sisowath Kossomak Nearirath (the Queen Mother) symbolizes in her person the permanence of the throne, but she does not reign."[4] Sihanouk has many times stated his intention never to reoccupy the throne, although in June, 1960, he became head of state, invested with monarchical authority. At the end of 1963, Sihanouk made known his desire that he be succeeded eventually by his son, Prince Naradipo, who is being educated in Peking. In 1966, he again insisted on Naradipo's succession. The chosen son is heir presumptive rather than political heir apparent.

Sihanouk administers his country formally through a cabinet that has responsibility to an elected national assembly. His chief political instrument is Sangkum, the party that has captured every seat contested in elections to the assembly since independence. The hierarchy of Sangkum, with Prince Sihanouk as its president, parallels that of the Cambodian Government; they are virtually the same in personnel. Membership in Sangkum is composed largely of public servants, who thus demonstrate their loyalty and ensure their continued employment. Sangkum provides the personnel for the key political institution in Cambodia—the National Congress—which meets as a popular forum in the capital every six months. In theory, this semiannual gathering provides an opportunity for Sangkum members and selected provincials to exercise control over the agents of government. In practice, the congress is an instrument used to demonstrate regard and affection for Sihanouk and further to secure his position in relation to leading members of the administration, whose political activity tends to be restricted to the office-seeking variety. At these congresses, members of the cabinet can be held up to public ridicule by Sihanouk for their errors and deviations, demonstrating publicly the accountability of government and his own position at the head of the political pecking order. Sangkum is in no sense a political party modeled on Western lines. It is a mass organization which, besides serving as the personal following of the head of state, seeks to include all facets of articulate Khmer opinion. Its object is to channel dissent into constructive forms. Sangkum has the advantage in this endeavor of providing the sole path to administrative and legislative office. This monopsony has facilitated political control, but has not enabled the government to check factional squabbling or the alarming incidence of corruption among public servants.

Sangkum is not always one big happy family. Organized in 1955 from diverse political elements, it still includes within its ranks a near microcosm of the political spectrum. It has, for example, a youthful left-wing faction, known colloquially as the Khmer Rose, which resents the activities of the rather large royal family. Younger members of the political elite, particularly those trained abroad, are inclined to expect meteoric rises in their careers rather than the slower pace of advance that is conventional in the West. Sihanouk has sought to accommodate youthful talent wherever possible, even up to the cabinet level. The experiment, however, has not been entirely successful, and he has demonstrated increasing concern with opposition that is often expressed in anti-monarchist form.

As far back as 1957, in an attempt to capture youthful enthusiasm and check disaffection, Sihanouk created the Royal Khmer
Socialist Youth.[5] This incongruous-sounding body is, in fact, the
junior section of Sangkum, and enrolls children of Sangkum members and those who make a good showing in the secondary
schools. The organization claims that its membership is now approaching 900,000. It has no competition, the Boy Scout Movement, for example, being banned. In practice, it provides a ready
pool of recruits to line routes and march in processions. The justification for the existence of such an organization was underlined
by an anti-Sangkum student riot in Siemreap in 1963.

Organized opposition existed outside Sangkum from its creation. The chief opposition group was the left-wing and pro-Communist Pracheachon, which drew its members from the anti-
French resistance and Cambodian or part-Cambodian affiliates of
the Viet-Minh. Until recently, the Pracheachon was allowed to
exist in a state of open proscription, where it could serve as a
convenient target for nationalist abuse. But during the past few
years Sihanouk, concerned with the trend of events in other parts
of Indochina, has taken pains to circumscribe the activities of the
Pracheachon; its current membership is estimated at less than
1,000. He is very anxious not to permit the growth of this body as
an effective alternative to the existing ruling group. Although
Sihanouk enjoys harmonious relations with foreign Communists,
he is determined to curtail the freedom of the Communists at
home. The country's domestic situation alone makes it exceed-
ingly difficult for the Cambodian Communists to spark any significant political protest, especially over international issues,
where Sihanouk has cut the ground from under their feet. He has
publicly warned Cambodia's Communists that he would throw
them out of the country unless they stopped conspiring against
the government. It would seem, however, that they are not completely dormant. In April, 1967, it was announced by Sihanouk
that armed Communists had attacked provincial guards in Battambang Province.

Another source of opposition, in clandestine form, is the Khmer

Serai (Free Cambodian Movement). This small group of disaffected republicans emanates from the anti-French resistance, but from its right wing, led by the exile Son Ngoc Thanh, who was Prime Minister after the Japanese-inspired declaration of independence in 1945. This group has been involved in plots against the regime and is believed to have received support from the governments in Saigon and Bangkok and from the CIA. Current activities of the Khmer Serai appear to be limited to minor incursions across the border and radio transmitting, which causes Sihanouk great personal annoyance. Because of the alleged association of this group with Cambodia's traditional enemies, the Thais and the Vietnamese, its activities are viewed with concern in Phnom Penh. It seems to be more of a nuisance, however, than a genuine threat.

In general, Cambodia appears to enjoy a real measure of political stability, which does not seem likely to be disturbed unduly in the immediate future. The prospects for continuing political stability appear to be linked to the government's ability to handle successfully the problems of the economy. In this sphere, Sihanouk is less gifted than in, for example, the realm of foreign policy. His popularity among the urban elite has lessened noticeably as a result of the progressive decline in the level of economic activity.

Such discontent has so far found no focus and rarely appears above the surface. The military, whose chief of staff, General Lon Nol, was Prime Minister from October, 1966, until April, 1967, when the Prince resumed the office, is the most obvious candidate for an alternative government; it has suffered the most from the rejection of American aid. The army's efficiency could be improved by standardization of its equipment, and the conditions of service of units along the borders are not too agreeable. But the bulk of the army is drawn from the peasantry, where Sihanouk has his strongest support and where, for the time being, in spite of difficulties, loyalty and dedication to the regime are sustained. Perhaps the regime's greatest assets are its clear title to govern and Sihanouk's leadership, regarded as indispensable in the absence of any practicable alternative. The head of state, Prince Norodom Sihanouk, may practice agitational politics to obtain, in part, the right kind of response from a people who are not always responsive, but he is undeniably a popular figure. This popularity, however, may well be a wasting asset if his indispensability cannot be passed on to a successor. For Sihanouk has pointed out, "As long as I am there, it's all right. But after me? I note with sadness that although the Cambodians may be united around me, I have not succeeded in uniting them amongst themselves."[6]

The Problem of Security

Since the Geneva Conference on Indochina formally sanctioned its independence in July, 1954, Cambodia has faced a security problem that had been in abeyance during the colonial period. After 1863, with the exception of the Japanese interlude from 1941-45, the French presence effectively safeguarded the Cambodians against encroachments by their traditional antagonists, the Thais and the Annamites (Vietnamese). After the withdrawal of the colonial power from the whole of Indochina, Cambodia had the ironic experience of being politically free yet territorially less secure. Thailand, its neighbor to the west and north, had revisionist aspirations to the bordering provinces of Battambang and Siemreap, which had been restored to Cambodia in 1946. To the east of Cambodia lay the southern portion of a truncated Viet-Nam. The more immediate concern of the regime in South Viet-Nam with the threat from North Viet-Nam had a restraining influence on its relations with Cambodia. The prospect of an eventual reunification of the two Viet-Nams, however, was fraught with danger for Cambodia. During the concluding stages of the Indochina War, Communist Viet-Minh forces had invaded Cambodia, although in insufficient strength to establish a foothold and so claim a voice in determining Cambodia's future at Geneva. An independent South Viet-Nam would be an uneasy neighbor. A reunified Viet-Nam controlled from Hanoi would mean the reappearance of traditional Vietnamese-Cambodian enmity in a vigorous and dynamic form.

Cambodia's traditional antagonists had powerful allies. Thailand and South Viet-Nam were closely associated with the United States. North Viet-Nam was aligned with the Soviet Union but more significantly with the bordering People's Republic of China, which exercised more than a peripheral presence in Southeast Asia. Quick to secure his country's advantage in exploiting this Cold War confrontation, Prince Sihanouk sought to use the opposing powers to establish a political equilibrium that would safeguard Cambodia's territorial and national integrity. What was known conventionally as neutralism for others, Sihanouk transcribed in distinctive form as neutrality for Cambodia—a dictate of geopolitical necessity. His rationale was as follows:

> Our neutrality has been imposed on us by necessity. A glance at a map of our part of the world will show that we are wedged in between two medium-sized nations of the Western bloc and only thinly screened by Laos from the scrutiny of two countries of the Eastern bloc, North Viet-Nam and the vast People's Republic of China. What choice have we but to try to maintain an equal balance between the "blocs." [7]

The practice of neutrality involved playing off the competing interests to Cambodia's advantage. Sihanouk viewed friendly relations with Communist China as a counter to any predatory ambitions of Thailand and South Viet-Nam. At the same time, he felt that a symbolic American presence together with economic assistance would help to maintain internal security and preserve a certain freedom of maneuver in dealing with Communist countries. Ties with Peking, he hoped, would also encourage restraint on the part of the North Vietnamese Government and the Cambodian left wing. In the same way, he expected that the United States would keep its allies in order.

Despite a somewhat tempestuous relationship with the United States, produced by a conviction that the U.S. approved of Thai and South Vietnamese activities against the Khmer state, Cambodia maintained a balance between East and West until the early 1960's. With the deterioration of the Western position, first in Laos and then in South Viet-Nam, Cambodian foreign policy changed and neutrality took on a new aspect. Cambodia wrote off the United States as an effective countervailing force in Indochina and began to believe that the only hope for political salvation was through the good offices of the government of the People's Republic of China. Convinced that it was inevitable that both Laos and Viet-Nam would be controlled by the regime in Hanoi, Sihanouk sought to secure his country's political future by aligning himself on foreign policy issues with Communist China and cutting, one by one, his ties with the United States. In this way, he hoped to avoid incorporation within the type of Indochinese People's Republic the Vietnamese Lao Dong (Communist) Party envisaged in its platform. Cambodia was to offer itself as a hostage to Chinese fortune. It is not clear exactly what relationship was envisaged for the future; but there was the prospect that an independent but obedient Cambodia would appeal more readily to Peking than a Cambodia incorporated into an Indochinese Communist state with Titoist pretensions. It should be pointed out that rigidity has never been a feature of Cambodian foreign policy. Ever hypersensitive to shifts in the balance of power in Southeast Asia, Cambodia can be expected to maneuver in any direction to preserve its national independence.

The guiding hand in Cambodian foreign policy is that of Sihanouk; he provides the inspiration and dynamic spirit for the conduct of his country's foreign relations. He articulates Cambodian hopes and fears and, if his actions and behavior are often regarded as bizarre and even outrageous outside his country, within Cambodia they are seen as eminently praiseworthy. Like another man he admires, French President Charles de Gaulle, Sihanouk speaks and acts as the embodiment of the nation. He no doubt satisfies a dual purpose in that role and merges his personal ambitions with national imperatives. Nevertheless, he manages to maintain a clear order of priorities, and the security of the nation is his chief objective.

2

The Emergence of
Independent Cambodia

On November 8, 1953, the King of Cambodia, Norodom Sihanouk, returned in triumph to Phnom Penh after several months of self-banishment, spent almost entirely within the borders of his kingdom. The appearance of the King in the capital indicated his satisfaction that the French Government, in agreements concluded with Cambodian representatives the previous August and October, had conceded the substance of Cambodian national demands. On the following day, Cambodia formally celebrated its independence, which has been commemorated every year since on November 9.

Cambodia secured its independence without a violent nationalist struggle. Militant local opposition to the French presence had existed since the restoration of colonial authority at the end of World War II, but it assumed only a fragmented form, lacking cohesion and unity of purpose. The principal challenge to the colonial power came from the externally directed Communist Viet-Minh, which had intervened physically in Cambodia and sought to exploit nationalist feeling and solicit popular support through its Khmer proxies. French concern at this prospect and its likely consequences for the conflict in Viet-Nam served the cause of Cambodian independence. Sihanouk used unconventional diplomatic methods to exploit this concern on behalf of Cambodian national aims at a propitious time. The young monarch (then only 31) traveled to a number of foreign capitals, displaying a zestful capacity for public relations, which he has utilized, often to excess, in his international dealings ever since. He exploited French anxieties about the situation in Indochina by arguing cogently that delay in granting genuine independence would encourage a popular drift away from the throne and toward the Cambodian associates of the Viet-Minh. French self-interest eventually dictated a positive response to Sihanouk's diplomatic initiatives. Today, these initiatives are regarded with reverence in Cambodia as the "Royal Crusade for Independence."

Historical Beginnings

Contemporary Cambodia traces its historical antecedents with some pride to the Empire of Kambuja, which emerged from Javanese suzerainty to reach its apogee around the twelfth and thirteenth centuries.[1] A sophisticated irrigation system provided the economic foundation for this political kingdom, whose legacy is the complex of monumental temples around the site of the capital at Angkor. The manner and style of temple building reflected an Indian cultural infusion which had taken root during earlier kingdoms and which shaped many forms of Khmer political and religious life. Most noteworthy among these was the divine status, deriving from the cosmo-magic cult of *deva-raja* (god-king), accorded to Khmer kings. The special reverence accorded to Prince Sihanouk by the Cambodian people today is an indication that belief in the divine qualities and sacred personality of kingship survives even in the twentieth century.

At its peak, the authority of Kambuja is believed to have extended from the Gulf of Siam to the Annamite Mountains and to have included the basins of the Menan Chao Phya and Mekong rivers. After the middle of the thirteenth century, the movement eastward of Thai (Siamese) peoples began to erode this position of dominance. Recurrent warfare caused the diversion of labor from construction projects to military purposes and, as a result, temple building halted and was never resumed. The Thais brought a new religion, a Sinhalese reform of Theravada Buddhism, which missionary monks from Ceylon had brought to Burma at the end of the twelfth century. Its simple and austere message had a popular appeal contrasting with the more remote court religions. The challenge to dogma assisted the crumbling of empire caused by internal dissension and by the excessive burden of royal extravagance. The failure of the hydraulics system, through a combination of neglect and Thai depredations, eventually made the capital site unsuitable for its purpose, and, in 1431, Angkor was abandoned.

Thereafter, the fortunes of the Khmer Empire declined. For nearly two centuries, Kambuja struggled to preserve its territorial integrity in the face of Thai pressure and internecine conflict. In 1603, the Thais reduced it to vassal status. The Cambodians, in association with the Annamites, removed Thai suzerainty seventeen years later, after a royal marriage with the Nguyên dynasty in Annam. Now encroachment also took place from the east. During the seventeenth century, the Annamites, who had moved south and extinguished the Kingdom of Champa, went on to annex the Mekong Delta region. By the nineteenth century, Cambodia, wedged between competing neighbors, preserved only a semblance of independent existence.

French Protectorate

France made its presence felt in Indochina during the middle of the nineteenth century by intervening in Annam on behalf of Christian missionaires. The goal of French intervention was to establish a position from which to exploit the legendary inland trade of China. The Cambodian King, Ang Duong, had solicited

French protection in 1854, but had been balked by the Siamese. When, in June, 1862, the Emperor of Annam ceded to France the three easterly provinces of what became known as Cochinchina, the French attempted to protect their acquisition by further expansion westward. In July, 1863, the French Governor of Cochinchina, Admiral de la Grandière, persuaded Ang Duong's son and successor, King Norodom, to accept a protectorate that would permit France to control external affairs and to install a resident-general in the capital. Despite Siamese attempts to forestall formal ratification, the accord came into effect in April of the following year. The disgruntled Siamese were appeased by a subsequent treaty (1867), whereby, in return for the surrender of its suzerain rights in Cambodia, France, on behalf of its ward, abandoned all claims to the westerly provinces of Battambang and Siemreap, which had been detached from Cambodia in 1795. (These territories were restored in 1907.)

France coerced Cambodia into another treaty in 1884, which established an authentic imperial relationship; in 1887, the protectorate was amalgamated with the protectorates of Laos, Tonkin, and Annam, the colony of Cochinchina, and the French leasehold in South China into the Union Indochinoise. At this time, France assumed complete control of Cambodian affairs. Local autonomy was replaced by direct rule under a system of residents, with ultimate authority in the hands of the Governor-General of the Union Indochinoise, stationed in Hanoi.

The major economic innovations arising from French rule —apart from slight improvements in public services, particularly in communications—were the establishment of rubber plantations and the recruitment of Vietnamese laborers to work them. Vietnamese were also introduced into the lower echelons of the civil administration. The Vietnamese, together with Chinese immigrants, soon began to play a dominant role in Cambodia's commercial life.

The new imperial relationship after 1884 produced automatic changes in the machinery of government, together with administrative and legal reforms. Popular participation in government was negligible. In 1913, a consultative assembly was established, but this institution was insignificant and no more than a place for preferment for obedient subjects of noble birth. If the throne was no longer omnipotent, its eminence remained unimpaired in the eyes of the predominantly rural population, which continued to venerate the king as the sacred living symbol of the god-king and protector of the Buddhist faith. The French, who were less interested in Cambodia than in Viet-Nam, sought to sustain this façade of monarchical power in the interests of preserving a stable government in a country where the pattern of traditional life was largely unaffected by colonial rule.

French rule may be described as exploitative and negligent, often rapacious.[2] Cambodians demonstrated opposition in the 1860's and 1880's, but thereafter the French administration had no serious internal security problem until the end of World War II. Authentic nationalist sentiment was not displayed until the 1930's, but the development of anything resembling an independence movement was overtaken by the events set in motion by international conflict.

Japanese Intervention

The beginning of the phase of Cambodia's political history that ended with the achievement of independence can be placed in June, 1940, with the fall of France. France's defeat by Germany undermined the French position in Indochina and made it possible for Japan to press its demands successfully on the Indochinese authorities. The Japanese were content to maintain the façade of French sovereignty and to permit the administration to continue its formal peacetime functions. In return, they enjoyed a preferred economic position and had the right to station troops in Indochina. Vichy French recognition of the economic and political supremacy of Japan in East Asia meant that Japan was the virtual master of Indochina. This was demonstrated in January, 1941, when the Japanese arranged the transfer of Cambodian and Laotian provinces to Thailand.

Toward the end of 1940, Japan had encouraged the Thai Government to reassert claims to Cambodian and Laotian provinces that had been removed from Thailand through French pressure in 1904 and 1907. The Governor-General of Indochina, supported by the Vichy Government, rejected these claims. The Thais defeated the French in the ensuing military engagement on Cambodian soil in January, 1941. The French regained the advantage, after a successful naval action in the Gulf of Siam, and the Japanese, who had already moved troops into Tonkin, intervened and forced an armistice. In March, the French signed a convention in Tokyo surrendering the disputed territories, including the greater part of the Cambodian provinces of Battambang and Siemreap. France's inability to fulfill its declared role as protector of Cambodia encouraged anti-French feeling in the country and effectively undermined the legitimacy of its colonial position.

By the end of 1941, Japan had deployed its troops in Cambodia as it inaugurated a campaign to strike southward against the Malay Peninsula and the Netherlands East Indies. Indochina served as a valuable means of supply for the prosecution of war, and, as long as this route was not threatened, the Japanese made no attempt to disturb the existing administrative framework. They reconsidered this policy, however, when the fortunes of armed conflict began to shift. The Japanese were alarmed at the increasing sympathies of the Indochinese administration toward the Free French Government of General de Gaulle and in October, 1944, when the Americans began landing in the Philippines, the Japanese were acutely concerned that the Indochina region was the next area marked for Allied liberation.

In March, 1945, the Japanese moved against the French administration throughout Indochina. Following the refusal of Governor-General Decoux to place all French forces and administrative agents under Japanese control, the Japanese staged a *coup de force* and on March 9 announced that Japan would support fully the long suppressed aspirations of the Indochinese for national independence.[3] On March 12, King Sihanouk proclaimed Cambodia's independence and began to form a government. The Japanese-controlled government interned all French civilians, and a number of political prisoners held by the French were released and sent back to Cambodia.

At the end of May, Son Ngoc Thanh, a part-Vietnamese born in Cochinchina, arrived from Japan to become Cambodian foreign minister. Formerly on the staff of the School of Advanced Pali Studies in Phnom Penh, Thanh was the leading exponent of nationalist sentiments during the 1930's. He had attracted some support among the younger, dissatisfied members of the educated elite and from Buddhist monks, who resented their diminished status. Together with an associate, Pach Chhoeun, Thanh founded the first Cambodian-language newspaper, *Nagaravatta,* in 1936. The publication had an openly anti-French orientation. During 1942, Buddhist discontent at decisions of the local French administration to try to Romanize the Khmer language and to adopt the Gregorian calendar was channeled into public protest following the arrest of a leading monk, Hem Chieu. Thanh became involved in an organized demonstration of Buddhist monks outside the French Residency. This act of protest led to disorder, and the French police intervened. Fearing arrest, Thanh fled to Bangkok, where the Japanese authorities arranged for him to go to Tokyo. He spent the war years in Japan, mainly involved in teaching, until the Japanese sponsored his return to Cambodia in 1945.[4]

Thanh served as Cambodian foreign minister until the Japanese surrender in the middle of August, 1945. He then obtained the arrest of his cabinet colleagues (though not the King) and installed himself as prime minister. His new cabinet included his former associate Pach Chhoeun and some members of the previous government. Thanh announced that he intended to uphold Cambodian independence, and the following month he organized a referendum on national independence, the results of which seemed to confirm his position; but his tenure of office did not last. On September 11, a French officer representing the Allied Command was parachuted into Phnom Penh, and with the imminent prospect of the return of the French, Thanh's authority was undermined. The traditional administrative elite and the court circles were in a mood to welcome the French, if only because they bitterly resented Thanh and the way he had come to power. They were fearful for their privileged status and suspicious of Thanh's Vietnamese affiliations. An opposition group secretly dispatched one of their number in Thanh's cabinet, Khim Tit, to Saigon to arrange with the French commander, Leclerc, for Thanh's arrest and removal. The British commander of the small Allied detachment sent to Cambodia encouraged this action.[5] On October 8, General Leclerc flew to Phnom Penh to arrest the Prime Minister personally. Thanh was taken to Saigon and charged with collaborating with the Japanese. He was sentenced to twenty years' hard labor, but the sentence was commuted to house arrest in France to forestall repercussions in Cambodia, where he still had a popular following. The King was officially uninvolved in this coup; the day of the arrest had been chosen to coincide with his absence on a pilgrimage.

With the arrival in Phnom Penh of a French commissioner and the King's affirmation of loyalty to France, the pre-1940 situation appeared restored, but a number of Thanh's supporters had retreated to the forests in the northwestern provinces. At the time, these provinces were still under the control of the "Free Thai" Government in Bangkok. Tolerated and even encouraged by the administration of Pridi Phanomyong, they established the Khmer Issarak (Free Cambodia) Movement to wrest independence from France by militant action. Pach Chhoeun formed a provisional government in exile and attempted to coordinate Issarak activities from Bangkok, but the insurgents proved unable to establish rapport between their disparate bands, whose motives ranged from genuine nationalism to plain brigandry. A government amnesty in Cambodia, the restoration of the northwestern provinces, and the assumption of power by Phibun Songkhram in Thailand caused a significant reduction in Issarak numbers by the end of 1947. Nevertheless, a core of dissidents remained to threaten security in the Thai border area. A source of insecurity in the southern part of the country was the activity of the Viet-Minh, drawing its support from among the Vietnamese minority and from persons of Khmer stock originating in Cochinchina.

A New Relationship with France?

The French officer who parachuted into Cambodia in September, 1945, lost little time in communicating with the Cambodian King. In three successive letters, he urged that a Cambodian delegation be sent to meet Admiral d'Argenlieu, the French High Commissioner for Indochina, to discuss the future status of Cambodia. In reply, the King agreed to negotiate but inquired whether the delegation would be considered to represent an independent country. He pointed out that his country had recovered its independence in March of that year and that relations with France would be considered only if they did not cast doubt on the independence of Cambodia.[6] The French authorities did not respond to this conditional acceptance, but their re-establishment in Phnom Penh indicated that they had no intention of recognizing the March 12 declaration of independence. Faced with *force majeur,* the King had no alternative but to wait and see what the French were prepared to offer.

The Brazzaville declaration of March 24, 1945, had indicated that de Gaulle's government was prepared to see changes in the formal *status quo ante.* Faced with the hostility of the United States, whose late President Roosevelt had objected to the restoration of French authority in Indochina, and also the determined opposition of the Viet-Minh in Viet-Nam, the French proposed formal constitutional concessions. On January 7, 1946, a *modus vivendi* agreement was concluded, which recognized Cambodia as an autonomous country within the Federation of Indochina.

Cambodia was to enjoy self-governing status within the limiting framework of the French Union, which approximated the British Commonwealth in form. In practice, the relationship did not differ radically from that based on the agreements of 1863 and 1884, which the *modus vivendi* was purported to have replaced. Real authority was to be in the hands of a French commissioner based in Phnom Penh, who was empowered to veto legislative acts and royal commands. France retained control over internal security and external relations, while certain federal matters, such as currency and customs, were to be handled in Saigon. Sovereignty rested with the so-called Federation of Indochina under the direction of the French High Commissioner.

The King agreed to accept France's offer of limited autonomy, because the alternative was a military struggle, which Cambodia was in no position to undertake and which would inflict unnecessary hardship on the population. Moreover, he felt that armed struggle against the French could work to the advantage of the Viet-Minh, whose success might result in a return to Vietnamese domination. Norodom Sihanouk commented at a later date: "To patronize bands of pirates, to open our frontiers to the Viet-Minh, so that, in the name of the struggle against France, they could massacre the people, and burn our bridges, houses, temples, schools, hospitals, inns, hotels, and towns—was this a patriotic solution acceptable to a king worthy of the name?" [7] He was also cautious because he was afraid that dissidence might in some way undermine the position of the throne. The King and the beneficiaries of the monarchy were conscious of their personal stake in Cambodia and were aware of the republican sympathies of Son Ngoc Thanh's supporters. An initial restoration of French rule was unavoidable, as Ho Chi Minh was also forced to concede in Viet-Nam. Cambodia had no means to resist French rule, and the King was not prepared to risk the unpredictable consequences of such action. Cambodia accepted French rule, but with some expectation that the French would grant further political concessions as a basis for future independence. [8]

For the time being, the King and his advisers saw greater advantage in participating in the negotiations scheduled to follow the signing of the *modus vivendi*. The agreement marked no major concession to Cambodian autonomy, but it did bring some practical benefits. The French had neglected educational facilities and had not attempted to create an indigenous administrative class until a few years before the beginning of World War II; at the end of the war, therefore, Cambodia was deficient in personnel trained in the skills necessary to administer even a miniature modern state. The transfer of limited powers provided an opportunity for Cambodians to gain new administrative experience. Educational opportunities were increased, with additional training available in Cambodia and in France. The French also promised to restore the Cambodian provinces that had come under Thai control in 1941; the promise was fulfilled by the Treaty of Washington, in November, 1946.

An Introduction to Popular Politics

Before World War II, political activity within Cambodia was restricted to internal and internecine disputes in the court and the royal family. The institutions of government created by the French provided for very limited participation and were without real authority. They served as agents of the corresponding levels of the French colonial administration and were designed to be rubber stamps, not instruments of political change.

A short period of Japanese-inspired independence (March-October) had stimulated growing political consciousness, and France's inability to perform her role of protector encouraged opposition to renewal of the imperial relationship. The end of the war thus brought a change in expectations, reflected most strongly among the members of a small but vigorous educated group that began returning from France just after the war. These circumstances had led, in turn, to a heightened awareness of the challenge to their position on the part of the court mandarinate and some members of the royal family. Meanwhile, not all of Son Ngoc Thanh's sympathizers had taken to the forests after his overthrow; those who remained in the capital soon had an opportunity to act within legal political bounds.

The King appeared sympathetic to demands for internal constitutional reform and sought to identify himself with the liberal sentiments of his generation. It is likely that Norodom Sihanouk's involvement in the reform movement was directly related to an interest in retaining his personal authority, although in changed circumstances. The French, for their part, were concerned to present the appearance of encouraging constitutional development. Looking back on those days, Prince Sihanouk has referred with some bitterness to what he describes as the French suggestion that he hand over his royalty to a handful of politicians.[9]

The French supervised plans for the termination of autocracy and a transition to a constitutional form of government. The surrender, in April, 1946, of Pach Chhoeun lent encouragement to prospects for political stability. A royal ordinance of the same date provided for fundamental civil liberties, and Cambodia's first political parties emerged in the following months. In announcing these innovations, the King made it known that he intended to introduce a constitution about which the people would be consulted. At the end of May, the government promulgated an electoral law to provide for the creation of a consultative assembly. This body was to be chosen directly by male suffrage through secret ballot and would consider proposals of the Franco-Khmer Constitutional Commission, which had been established at the end of 1945.

Two main political associations competed in the elections to the Consultative Assembly. Their programs reflected fairly accurately the division of the Cambodian political elite.[10] The Liberal Party, led by Prince Norindeth, was conservative in outlook and drew its active support from the more senior public servants, the courtier class, and the small group of landowners. The Liberals tended to favor gradual political change, with representation based on a more restricted suffrage than that which was to elect the Consultative Assembly. The party was equally moderate in its views on Cambodia's relationship with France; the supporters of the Liberal Party had more reason than most to expect personal benefit from continuation of French rule. Insofar as France underpinned a traditional political and social order, the Liberals stood to gain; they would suffer most from any radical discontinuity.

The chief opposition to the Liberals came from the Democratic Party, which attracted the support of the younger generation of educated Cambodians. The Democrats were led by Prince Youtevong, who had spent many years studying in France and had returned with keen desire to transplant the French parliamentary system onto Cambodian soil. The Democratic Party attracted strong support from junior officials, schoolteachers, and the semi-educated, who saw themselves as non-beneficiaries of the existing system. By and large, its members were ambitious and even angry young men in a hurry; the generational gap was certainly one distinguishing feature between the two major parties. Its numbers were augmented by followers of Son Ngoc Thanh, who came to represent the most radical view on political change, and the party won sympathy from some of the non-voting but influential Buddhist monks. While not explicitly anti-monarchist, the Democratic Party aimed to restrict the throne to a formal constitutional position. It sought, above all, a sovereign parliament unhindered by royal prerogative.

There can be no doubt that the King viewed the Democrats' program with some apprehension. When he sanctioned proposals for constitutional reform, he did not envisage the same reduction in his personal authority as did the Democrats. Given the increased autonomy of the Cambodian Government within the restrictions set by the French, he may even have expected to exercise more power as the constitutional system developed.

A third, but insignificant, contestant in the elections was the Progressive Democratic Party, led by Prince Norodom Montana, who enjoyed a limited personal following.

One cannot fail to notice that all three political parties were led by members of the royal family.

The elections took place in September, 1946. A decisive factor in the outcome in the provinces was the influence of public officials in favor of the Democratic Party, while rumors of French support tended to be a disadvantage to the Liberals. The assembly that resulted from these elections was very conscious of its representative status. The Democrats received fifty seats to the Liberals' sixteen, and three seats went to independents; the Progressive Democrats won no seats at all. The Democratic majority had no doubts about its competence on constitutional matters.

The Cambodian representatives in the Franco-Khmer Constitutional Commission sympathized with the outlook of the Liberal Party, and the constitutional proposals that emerged from their deliberations reflected the Liberals' views. Chief among these were proposals that future assemblies be elected on the basis of a more restricted franchise and that executive authority be shared between the King and the Cabinet. The Assembly refused to approve such proposals, which the Democratic majority regarded as a regression. The members of the Assembly were in no mood to vote away the fruits of power, which they believed to be within an inch of plucking. They considered the basis upon which they had been elected reason enough to reject their formal consultative status and to assume instead a genuine constitutional role.

Despite the King's efforts, the Assembly rejected the proposals of the Franco-Khmer Commission and created its own constitution, adopting, of course, the principles of the Democratic Party. The Constitution—modeled on French practice and completely alien to Cambodian experience—was promulgated in May, 1947. It continued the system of representation that had brought the Democratic Party to power and endowed the King with the ceremonial functions of a constitutional monarch. A certain ambiguity in the wording of the Constitution, however, obscured the formal prerogatives of the sovereign. Article 21, which stated that all powers emanated from the King, exemplified this lack of clarity. Because of Cambodia's strong tradition of monarchical supremacy, the King was later able to interpret to his own advantage this article and others relating to the dissolution of the Assembly and the choice of the Prime Minister. For the time being, however, the King was prepared to accept the Constitution rather than set aside by authoritarian means the new electorally sanctioned political institutions.

During 1947, the Democratic Party continued to control the Assembly, augmenting its active support by granting an amnesty to the Issaraks in April. The Issaraks who returned—estimated at approximately 3,000—tended to associate themselves with the aims of the Democratic Party. The death of Prince Youtevong was a turning point. A man of outstanding ability, if excessively idealistic, he had been able to exercise a unifying influence on the factions that made up the Democratic Party. After his death, Issarak sympathizers tended to dominate the activities of the party.

The first Assembly had been given a consultative role, but had formed itself into a constituent assembly. With the promulgation of the new constitution, it had lost its original *raison d'être*, and arrangements were made to hold fresh elections. When the elections took place in December, the Democratic Party once again polled a majority of the votes, gaining fifty-four of the total of seventy-five seats in an Assembly that was to serve for four years. The new Assembly met in January, 1948, now under the influence of the activist wing of the Democratic Party, and personal feuds and self-seeking were prominent features of its parliamentary practice. The Democrats seemed unable to provide stable leadership; their first government fell after a vote of no confidence in August. The second government lasted only a few months; it collapsed after the formation of a dissident faction within the Democratic Party led by Yem Sambaur, a Cabinet member. Governmental instability was combined with consistent obstruction of legislation proposed by the King.

After a succession of false starts, the Democrats succeeded in forming a new cabinet with Liberal support in February, 1949.

Yem Sambaur became the new Prime Minister and began a vigorous campaign against corruption in public life, which did not endear him to the Assembly. Difficulty arose over the negotiations redefining the status of Cambodia and its future relationship with France. At the end of 1948, the King had received a letter from the President of France proclaiming the independence of Cambodia within the French Union. The letter stated that this independence had no limits other than those imposed by membership in the French Union. To the Democrats, membership in the French Union and Cambodian independence were contradictory. They were, therefore, opposed to negotiations that had the object of formally sanctioning Cambodia's subject relationship to France. Determined to use their power in the Assembly to block the ratification of any treaty that embodied such provisions, the Democrats opposed the continuation of Yem Sambaur as Prime Minister and sought to undermine his position by inspiring defection from the Cabinet. Only one member was persuaded to submit his resignation. When this minister was not replaced and the government continued as if nothing had happened, open conflict broke out between the Democrats and Yem Sambaur. Finally, when the Assembly approved a motion censuring him, Yem Sambaur obtained royal consent to dissolve the Assembly.

These events proved fortuitous for the King, who had become increasingly concerned about the prospects for ratification of the Franco-Khmer Treaty. He decided not to call for new elections, justifying his decision on the practical ground that increased Issarak and Viet-Minh activity had caused a progressive deterioration in public security. Instead of calling new elections, he appointed a provisional government, with Yem Sambaur as Prime Minister.

The Franco-Khmer Treaty of November, 1949

The King's attitude toward the question of independence was essentially pragmatic. He was well aware of the immediate consequence of a national uprising and he saw no reason, for personal or national advantage, to risk the limited autonomy Cambodia had already gained in any vainglorious move against the French. Although he had pointed out to the French Commissioner for Cambodia in 1948 that only complete independence would provide the solution to Franco-Cambodian differences, the Commissioner's negative response forced Sihanouk to continue trying to alter his country's status in piecemeal fashion.

The following year, during negotiations with the French High Commissioner in Indochina, Sihanouk sought assurances that the proposed treaty redefining Cambodia's status would provide for genuine internal sovereignty and that Cambodian independence recognized by France would have international significance. Sihanouk sought recognition by the principal powers so that Cambodia would have diplomatic representation abroad and could participate in the United Nations. He requested further assurances that military zones under the control of French forces would be progressively reduced by the establishment of pacification areas under exclusive Cambodian control and command. Finally, he asked the French Government to agree to an amnesty for those Issaraks who would surrender and for political exiles, particularly Son Ngoc Thanh. The French High Commissioner readily gave assurances to increase Cambodian autonomy, but he would not concede total independence. An exchange of letters brought the treaty into being in November.

By the terms of the treaty, France recognized Cambodia as an independent state and formally abrogated the agreements relating to the protectorate. Independence was qualified; France retained control over certain aspects of the judicial system and the economy and complete control of military operations in time of war in addition to the right to maintain bases in Cambodia. Provisions requiring the coordination of foreign policy with the policies adopted by the High Council of the French Union restricted Cambodia's freedom in the conduct of its foreign relations. This meant that the French Government had to approve any international agreement specifically involving Cambodia.

Economic questions not covered by the treaty were considered at the Pau Conference, June to November, 1950. The Conference defined the federal powers of the associated states of Indochina. The agreement that resulted from the Pau Conference permitted Cambodia to control its own foreign trade and finance, while customs and telecommunications were to be handled by boards composed of the associated states of Indochina. The Pau discussions brought out many differences of opinion between Cambodians and Vietnamese.

Cambodia was now an associated state within the French Union. This dubious accomplishment brought it diplomatic recognition from the major Western powers, but from only South Korea and Thailand among the Asian nations. Cambodia also secured admission to some of the agencies of the United Nations; it did not attain formal membership in the organization until 1955.

The French had begun evacuating troops from the provinces of Kompong Thom and Siemreap even before the treaty was signed. The establishment of a Cambodian national army under the provisions of the treaty made it possible to conduct pacification operations in Issarak areas without the odium attached to association with the French. Autonomous Cambodian units were able to act as agents of an ostensibly self-governing state, and thus to solicit and receive popular support. The surrender in September, 1949, of Dap Chhuon Machulpich, who since 1946 had been the leader of the Khmer Committee of National Liberation, was a notable success for the King. Machulpich had built up a large personal following in Siemreap, where he enjoyed warlord status. The King felt that Machulpich's surrender justified demanding an extension of autonomous areas for Cambodian forces, but the French—concerned with Viet-Minh activity—transferred only the province of Battambang to Cambodian control in 1951.

The King regarded the Franco-Khmer Treaty as a means to an end. In his own words, it was a "springboard" from which to achieve complete independence.[11] He felt that France, by conceding formal independence, would find it increasingly difficult to refuse further concessions. For the immediate future, it was necessary to face the growing Viet-Minh threat, and for that purpose French help was an unavoidable evil.

This order of priorities was not acceptable to the Democratic Party, whose radical wing was becoming increasingly vociferous in denouncing the treaty as a mockery of independence. This argument was lent substance by Cambodia's membership in the the French Union, which also included representatives of French colonial territories. The King further alienated the Democrats by seeking to make changes in the Constitution to ensure the Assembly's approval of the treaty. He finally decided to implement the agreement through a series of ratification protocols, thus avoiding the necessity of calling an assembly.

Internal political dissension continued. The assassination in January, 1950, of Ieu Koeus, a former prime minister, increased the Democrats' suspicion of Yem Sambaur, whom they had criticized bitterly for his handling of a strike by schoolchildren. In May, Yem Sambaur resigned, after France had attempted to dilute its treaty concessions. The King took over the office of prime minister, hoping to establish a coalition government. Within a month, he had relinquished the post to his uncle, Prince Monipong, who continued to rule without the Assembly until February, 1951. During his tenure of office, Cambodia and France signed the Pau Agreement, augmenting Cambodia's financial and fiscal autonomy. This agreement led to increased criticism of the regime, because it placed key governmental powers under federal control, rather than in the hands of Cambodian ministers. At the same time, agitation continued for a return to normal parliamentary life. A general deterioration in economic activity gave the Democrats further cause for complaint. It was not difficult to demonstrate the defects of so-called independence and to denounce the government for all shortcomings. In September, following yet another change of prime minister, the King decided to hold general elections for a new assembly. The prospect of a fresh start and the accompanying hope that this would engender a sense of responsibility among his opponents was fundamental to the King's decision in this matter.

New Elections

In the 1951 elections, nine parties put up candidates, but the results were similar to those of 1947. Once more the Democratic Party, with its efficient organization, won control of the Assembly. The Liberals again took second place. The only minor party to make any impression was the Northeast Victorious, whose four seats included three in Siemreap, where its leader, the former Issarak Dap Chhuon Machulpich, was very influential. A significant feature of the election was the high level of abstentions, which probably reflected popular indifference in the provinces as well as the state of public security.

In October, the King appointed Huy Kanthoul to head a new cabinet. The re-establishment of the parliamentary system wrought no essential change in political behavior. The basic conflict between the Democrats and the King was as deeply rooted as ever. The first official act of the new government—reshuffling of the civil service according to criteria of party loyalty—did not augur well for a compatible relationship between the throne and the government.

At this point, the return of Son Ngoc Thanh introduced a new element into the political arena. Sihanouk obtained Son Ngoc Thanh's release from France in the hope that such a gesture would conciliate opponents of the throne. He claims to have been responsible for persuading French authorities to commute Thanh's sentence in 1945 and also claims to have sought an amnesty for him during the negotiations for the Franco-Khmer Treaty, writing no less than four letters on Thanh's behalf between October, 1949, and March, 1951.[12] Thanh returned to Phnom Penh at the end of October, 1951, and one of his first acts was to write to the King expressing his gratitude and loyalty. There then seemed every prospect that he would be offered a post in the government.

Thanh had been received on his return by tumultuous popular acclaim. His reception was also a demonstration against the French; the preceding day, the French Commissioner in Cambodia, Jean de Raymond, had been murdered by his Vietnamese manservant. It is likely that Thanh was unduly flattered by his reception, which certainly contrasted with the diminishing popularity of the King in the capital.[13] He may have felt that the public mood was ripe for agitation to his own advantage. He was, no doubt, still a sincere nationalist, and the temper of anti-French feeling in the capital must also have motivated his actions. He probably saw little prospect for genuine independence through the limited constitutional process permitted in Cambodia, and he may thus have decided that militant action was necessary. There is also a possibility that he had anticipated being invited to form a government on his return and did not relish the prospect of serving in a subordinate position.

In December, Thanh announced publicly that only the departure of French troops could assure the independence of Cambodia and restore peace and order. He began publishing a newspaper called *Khmer Krok* (*Cambodians Awake*), which sought to arouse popular feeling against the French. When the paper was suspended in February, 1952, Thanh fled the capital and sought refuge with the Issaraks along the Thai border. On March 9, the anniversary of the Japanese *coup de force* in Indochina, he broadcast from his forest headquarters that he was leading the resistance against French rule and at the same time expressed his republican sympathies. He recognized that the throne would be a continual obstacle to the exercise of power by any popular representative. Thanh confined his activities to those provinces under the autonomous military control of Cambodian troops, avoiding parts of the country that were still under French military command.

Thanh's flight aggravated the political situation in Phnom Penh and increased the differences between the King and all those who desired genuine independence. Large student demonstrations erupted, and political activity became increasingly factional. The Democratic Party was divided between those who wished to preserve the monarchy and those who supported Thanh and a republican system. The King and the French authorities suspected the Democratic leadership of having connived to arrange the flight of Thanh. The Democratic Party lent substance to these suspicions by the equivocal stand it took against the Issaraks, who were reinvigorated by the appearance of a new leader (Thanh). The King, finding the situation more and more intolerable, now saw the Democratic Party as a direct threat to his personal position. When the Democratic Government of Huy Kanthoul ordered the arrest of Yem Sambaur in June, 1952, the King—already under pressure from the French not to make any concessions to the Democrats—seized the opportunity to dismiss Huy Kanthoul and again assume the office of Prime Minister. He then announced publicly that he intended to assume full powers for three years to implement a program of national pacification. More important, he declared that he would seek a full and satisfactory independence, on which the people would later have an opportunity to pass judgment.

The flight of Thanh and its political repercussions had made the King uncomfortably aware that the people had come to view his gradualist approach to the question of independence as a sacrifice of national rights. His views on the relationship between Cambodia and France had marked him as too compromising and thus cast doubt on his patriotism. Even a monarchy as firmly rooted in tradition as Cambodia's could not hope to survive if there was a popular feeling that it was acting as the servant of a colonial power. To maintain its authority, the monarchy had to associate itself with the protection of national interests. Sihanouk's apparent failings on this score had encouraged support for those in the Democratic Party who favored the establishment of a republic and for those who supported Son Ngoc Thanh. It became increasingly evident that national unity could be restored and political malaise removed only if the King were to associate himself with uncompromising demands for complete independence from France. He would also have to make it clear that he could control the course of political events by proving that independence could be achieved without the help of Issarak activity. The King's anxiety increased as a result of evidence that the Communist Viet-Minh had sought to provide a legitimate stand for its activities in Cambodia abetted by some Issarak bands. In April, 1950, the Viet-Minh established a Central Committee for the Liberation of the Khmer People. This was the first step in a campaign to set up the formal apparatus that would ensure Viet-Minh participation in decisions relating to the political future of Cambodia. By March of the following year, the Viet-Minh had succeeded in creating a United Front of Khmer Issarak, Neo Lao Issarak, and Viet-Minh, and, by November, a Cambodian revolutionary party, whose organizational charter was a simplified and expurgated version of the statute of the Vietnamese Lao Dong (Communist) Party.[14]

These activities were initiated by the *Bureau central sud,* led by a part-Khmer, Sieu Heng, who was responsible for preparing the administrative infrastructure for Viet-Minh activities in Cambodia. In 1952, the Khmer Committee of National Liberation revised its name and function, becoming the Khmer Resistance Government, headed by Son Ngoc Minh, a possibly fictitious character, often purported to be a brother of Son Ngoc Thanh. This so-called government was recognized only by the Pathet Lao and the Government of the Democratic Republic of Viet-Nam, which sought to sponsor its protégé at the Geneva Conference on Indochina in 1954.

The King had good reason for believing that it was urgent to convince his people of his patriotism and to demonstrate that he was more concerned with Cambodia's independence than the insurgents. He first sought the approval of the Assembly for his intention to assume full powers for three years, but that body refused to take a position, which was equivalent to expressing a negative vote. The activist wing of the Democrats then sought to encourage dissidence and unrest among students, soldiers, and Buddhist monks. In January, 1953, following the Assembly's refusal to approve the budget, the King dissolved the chamber and declared a state of national emergency. This provided the government with extraordinary powers, which it used to arrest a number of people, including four former ministers and twelve deputies. On January 29, the King appointed a National Consultative Council; then, after installing his father as regent and head of the council, Sihanouk left for Europe to begin his crusade for independence.

The Royal Crusade

In his message of June 15, 1952, the King committed himself to achieving complete independence within three years and transferring to his own jurisdiction those prerogatives exercised by France that limited the sovereignty of his country. In particular, he sought full judicial competence, military autonomy, and revision of the agreements that placed economic control in the hands of Indochinese federal authorities. In February, 1953, accompanied by Prime Minister Penn Nouth, the King set off ostensibly for a holiday in Italy but actually to establish himself eventually at La Napoule on the French Riviera.

On March 5, he wrote to French President Auriol demanding full sovereignty for Cambodia. In his letter, Sihanouk pointed out that he had tried to persuade his countrymen to have confidence in French promises that they would win independence as soon as they had pacified the Viet-Minh. He explained that these attempts at persuasion could carry no weight while certain anomalies existed in judicial, military, and economic matters and went on to say that France could not count on complete popular support until Cambodia became a sovereign state. He emphasized that the Cambodian people did not support the French struggle against the Viet-Minh; they were not convinced of its utility. He also referred to the prospect of the monarchy disappearing in the face of attractive republican, if not Communist, sentiment among the younger generation. Sihanouk had to send a second letter in the same vein before he received a reply inviting him to a meeting in Paris at the end of March. No positive results emerged from his conversations with the French President, and there was every indication that his claims were being politely but pointedly ignored. On April 3, the King sent a memorandum to the French Government reiterating his demands. He subsequently saw Letourneau, the minister in charge of the Associated States, who led Sihanouk to understand that his démarches were inopportune and advised him to return to his capital, hinting that if he did not he might be removed from the throne.

It was apparent that the King had not been able to secure the slightest promise of concessions from the French Government. He therefore sought to make his case as public as possible to attract international support and to embarrass the French. He went from France to Ottawa, where he held a press conference on April 12 and drew attention to the related problems of fighting the Communists and satisfying the aspirations of the Cambodian people for independence. He pointed out that Cambodia would have to enjoy unconditional and unquestioned sovereignty in order to remove the insecurity fomented by the Issaraks and the Viet-Minh. He argued that the Issaraks and the Viet-Minh had an increasing prospect of attracting popular support as long as they could claim to fight for liberation and independence. Only by providing Cambodia with real independence could the problems of security be adequately tackled. If the people felt they were being asked to support the continuation of French control, it was no wonder they found the Issaraks and the Viet-Minh an attractive alternative.[15] The King went on from Canada to the United States, where he had what he has described as a disappointing interview with Secretary of State John Foster Dulles. Dulles did not appear to share Sihanouk's conviction that freedom from French tutelage would provide sufficient incentive to check Communist advances. He merely promised to persuade France to grant total independence after the Communist menace had been destroyed.

The King made his greatest impact in the United States with an interview published in *The New York Times*,[16] which received wide publicity abroad. During this interview, he returned to the theme that withholding independence would result in a popular movement away from his government into the arms of the Communist-led Viet-Minh. He added cogency to his remarks by referring to the situation in Laos, which had suffered a large-scale Viet-Minh penetration earlier in the same month and by pointing out that he was not certain whether he had the authority to call for general mobilization in similar circumstances. (France's inability to protect Laos certainly helped eventually to undermine its position in neighboring Cambodia.) Sihanouk went on to demand, as the price of remaining in the French Union, the same relationship as that which existed between Britain and the independent members of the Commonwealth.

The French response to the excessive publicity given the Cambodian case was to invite Prime Minister Penn Nouth for discussions in Paris on April 25. The King, in the meantime, went on to Japan, where he remained to await the results of the Paris meeting. On May 9, Penn Nouth entered into an agreement on behalf of the Cambodian Government slightly modifying the existing status of Cambodia. The limited concessions were far from satisfactory to the King. For example, while France conceded that the King should be the commander-in-chief of the Cambodian Army, authority was not extended in the military zones. Cambodia was to be allowed to make independent decisions in economic affairs, but only with the prior approval of the Associated States. On one issue of immediate impact the French refused to budge. They would not accept prior Cambodian approval before altering the exchange rate of the piastre (the currency unit of the Associated States). On May 10, devaluation took place.

On May 14, the King returned to Cambodia with little to show for his labors, but his efforts were rewarded internally. As a result of his attempts to secure more complete independence, Issarak bands began to come over to the side of the government and were willing to integrate their forces into the national army. With this surrender, the King modified the emergency measures and announced clemency for those involved. He was still dissatisfied, however, with the popular response to his activities, particularly after a tour of military units in the Northwest, where he continued to encounter the feeling that by compromising with France he had obstructed the achievement of independence.

On June 12, the King decided to make another dramatic move. He handed over full powers to Prime Minister Penn Nouth and left for Thailand. His motives were again to alert public opinion to his patriotic intent and to embarrass the French. His decision to go into exile was prompted by continuing uncertainty as to whether he could provide a sufficiently attractive alternative to the appeal of the Issaraks and the Viet-Minh. His visit to the Northwest had aroused his anxieties on this score, and he therefore felt the need to try to outbid those who claimed to be fighting for the nationalist cause. He may also have acted out of concern that the French would try to depose him as they had the King of Morocco. He probably chose Thailand for his voluntary exile because, except for South Korea, Thailand was the only Asian country that had accorded Cambodia diplomatic recognition. In addition, the full complement of Western diplomatic missions in Bangkok afforded great possibilities for recruiting support for his objectives.

The King found a lukewarm, if not hostile, reception in Bangkok. The Thai Government—having no desire for bad relations with France and feeling patronizing toward Cambodia and its King—informed Sihanouk's secretariat that he could be considered only as an inconvenient political refugee. The Thais insisted that he had no right to engage in any political activity. He was forbidden to stay at his country's legation and was confined almost incommunicado at a hotel. The attitude of the Thai Government at this time left a bitterness that certainly contributed to future unhappy relations between the two neighboring countries.[17]

Disgruntled at what he felt was shabby treatment on the part of the Thais, Sihanouk returned to Cambodia, but not to Phnom Penh. He established himself in the province of Battambang, then under the autonomous control of Cambodian troops. The King vowed to remain out of the capital until France had satisfied his terms for independence. This move heightened tension in Phnom Penh, where the French authorities reacted by moving in troops to protect French lives. On June 28, Sihanouk ordered a general mobilization; the response to his call indicated that he enjoyed increasing popular support. Three groups of Issaraks not associated with the Viet-Minh rallied behind Sihanouk, and Cambodians serving in French units left their regiments to join the King. The decision of students at the Cambodian military academy to leave college to join their King in the Northwest was an indication of his changed relationship with the younger generation.

The French faced increasing difficulties both in the war in Viet-Nam and at home. By May, the Viet-Minh forces had advanced well into Laos, stopping only a few miles from the royal capital of Luang Prabang. After demonstrating French inability to defend the country, the Viet-Minh returned to the province of Sam Neua, where they installed the Pathet Lao Resistance Government. In France, several weeks of interegnum and crisis followed the fall of the René Mayer Government in May. At the end of June, Joseph Laniel became Prime Minister of France. He acted immediately to bolster the situation in Indochina, making some cabinet changes relating to the Associated States and dismissing Letourneau, who had become very unpopular in Cambodia. On July 3, Laniel announced to the governments of the three Associated States that France was ready to complete their independence by transferring residual powers. Cambodia immediately put up proposals suggesting French recognition of full independence and sovereignty and reiterating previous demands relating to judicial competence, military autonomy, and economic sovereignty. After discussions at the end of July, the Cambodian Government agreed to restrict its immediate demands to a transfer of powers over the army, police,

and judiciary. The French then promised to settle matters relating to finance, customs, and currency in subsequent discussions.

On August 29, France transferred to Cambodia control over the
judiciary and the police. Difficulties then arose over the command
of five Cambodian battalions that the French wanted to use in Viet-
Nam. A radio speech by Prime Minister Penn Nouth on September
10—probably designed to pressure the French—radically altered
the negotiating situation by involving the United States, which
had provided Cambodia with $25 million in aid since 1951. In the
speech, Penn Nouth pointed out that the Cambodian people and
Buddhist clergy had no desire for Communism, but they would not
become involved against the Viet-Minh providing that Cambodia
were left alone.[18] The prospect of a neutral Cambodia alarmed the
United States, whose chargé d'affaires warned the Cambodian
Government that Congress would cut off aid to Cambodia if the
speech was interpreted as a declaration of neutralism. Senate Republican Majority Leader William F. Knowland was then visiting
Indochina, and he postponed his intended visit to Phnom Penh
when informed of the content of the speech. Penn Nouth sent immediate assurances to Knowland, seeking to explain away his statement as a stratagem to demonstrate to the Cambodian people that
the Viet-Minh had no intention of withdrawing its troops from
Cambodia. It is not clear whether Penn Nouth had indicated by his
speech the seeds of what was later to become a credo of Cambodian foreign policy. At the time, the Viet-Minh threat showed no
sign of receding, and, to all intents and purpose, Cambodia was
faced with the prospect of sharing a common border with a country
increasingly under Communist control. It is more likely that the
speech was related to the negotiations with the French. It is also
possible to regard the government's subsequent statement that
Cambodia was not ready to join in the struggle against Communism as part of its bargaining to secure formal control of the Cambodian forces. The point has been well made that during the following year, when Viet-Minh pressure intensified, Cambodia was

the most anxious of the three Indochina states to associate itself militarily within the United States.[19] In late 1953, the Geneva Conference was still some months in the future, and the Cambodian Government could not know what kind of political settlement would be effected in Indochina. In September, 1953, Cambodia was threatened by the Viet-Minh, and the most that one can say of Penn Nouth's initiative is that it anticipated, with faint hope, a Viet-Minh concession. It was many months later, toward the end of 1954 and after the Geneva settlement, that the word "neutralism" began to find favor in the Cambodian capital.

By mid-September, 1953, Cambodia and France had reached an agreement whereby France would command three battalions of Cambodian troops. Discussions on the use of the troops prolonged the negotiations until October 17, when they reached a settlement that was satisfactory to the Cambodian Government. Following the successful conclusion of negotiations on subjects to which he had committed himself, Sihanouk returned to his capital on November 8. He received a triumphant welcome, which vindicated his somewhat unconventional methods. The following day, Cambodia officially celebrated its independence. Meanwhile, France and Cambodia continued to negotiate the transfer of the residual economic powers, but they did not reach a satisfactory agreement until the end of December, 1954.

The King returned to an unstable political situation. Conflict developed immediately between the government in Phnom Penh and those who had been in exile with the King. Within a week, a coalition government was established that included left-wing Democrats. In spite of the King's apparent success, the appeal of Son Ngoc Thanh and the opposition of the Democrats were still important factors in the political situation. The King found it necessary to threaten abdication if the opposition did not cease its attempts to minimize his role in the independence struggle. In December, the King returned to the Northwest, the scene of his earlier triumph, to lead operations against remaining dissidents. This tactic appeared to quiet the opposition.

Sihanouk's position improved at the beginning of 1954, with the surrender of Issaraks in progressively large numbers; Son Ngoc Thanh remained in his forest retreat and refused to concede the success of the King. It became increasingly apparent that Sihanouk had so far been only partially successful in winning over the dissidents. He was unable to achieve a more general recognition until the Indochina settlement was concluded at the Geneva Conference in July, 1954.

The King's success in gaining concessions from the French was only a partial contribution to the restoration of political stability. He had helped Cambodia achieve the required forms of independence with French recognition of its judicial and military competence, but he had not succeeded in removing threats to its independent existence. The situation in the capital had improved, and increasing numbers of Issaraks from the Northwest region had indicated a willingness to surrender, but the problem of the Viet-Minh had, by January, 1954, assumed menacing proportions. On April 2, three battalions of regular Viet-Minh forces invaded Cambodia from Laos, along the northeastern frontier. They also attacked the Phnom Penh-Battambang train and killed more than one hundred Cambodians. The Viet-Minh intervention coincided with the siege of Dien Bien Phu and probably had a diversionary purpose. As a tactical move, it certainly had a broader objective— the establishment of a secure territorial base within Cambodia before the international discussions on Indochina scheduled to begin in Geneva on April 26.

Cambodia immediately dispatched troops to the troubled area to deal with the situation, but the Cambodian response was not sufficient to enforce a total withdrawal of the Viet-Minh, whose irregular forces had been ensconced in the country since at least 1951. It is perhaps surprising that the Cambodian Government waited until April 23 to inform the United Nations of the Viet-Minh invasion and until May 20 to request military assistance from the United States.[20] This lapse of about seven weeks between the Viet-Minh penetration and the eventual call for American aid would seem to indicate that there was no direct connection between the two events. The fall of Dien Bien Phu—which raised the prospect of a general French collapse in Indochina—and the Communist powers' demand for the recognition and representation of the so-called Khmer Resistance Government during the initial weeks of the Geneva Conference were probably more decisive factors in the request for United States military aid. The Cambodian Government must have felt a desperate need for a great power guarantee, which could come only from the West and, more specifically, the United States.[21] Indeed, until the implementation of the Geneva Accords—and the consequent recession of the Viet-Minh threat—the Cambodian Government gave every indication that it would pursue a Western-oriented foreign policy.

By the time Cambodia requested assistance from the United States Government, Washington no longer felt it was urgent to take drastic measures in Indochina. In April, Secretary of State Dulles had sought to persuade the British Government to intervene militarily to rescue the beleaguered French garrison at Dien Bien Phu. He was unable to convince the British Government that the kind of attack he envisaged—a carrier-based nuclear strike—was suitable to the occasion.[22] British Foreign Secretary Anthony Eden was most reluctant to involve his country in a general war in Indochina and "probably later American action against the Chinese mainland." [23] He was also anxious to avoid any action likely to prejudice the success of the forthcoming Geneva Conference on Indochina. Dulles hoped that Anglo-American governmental harmony on military action in Indochina would encourage faint hearts in Congress and outside to approve of such a course. In any event, Congressional resistance, unrelated to British objections, plus determined opposition by the American military[24] forced a re-appraisal of the situation.[25] Dien Bien Phu fell on May 7 and, expecting that Indochina would have to be written off to the Communists, the United States turned its attention to attempting to shore up the rest of Southeast Asia through a defensive alliance.

After the first few days of the Geneva Conference, Dulles no longer expressed the same anxiety about Indochina. His changed state of mind did not augur a positive response to Cambodia's request for American military assistance. At a press conference on May 11, Dulles went so far as to refute the "domino theory" (successive states falling to Communism) that President Eisenhower had expounded the previous month. Dulles claimed that Viet-Nam was not necessarily vital to the defense of Southeast Asia and that Laos and Cambodia, though important, were not essential to this purpose.[26] The fact that the Cambodian Government was prepared to make a serious request for assistance in the light of this speech indicated its limited alternatives and its desperation. Until the Communist concessions at Geneva in late June, the Viet-Minh threat to Cambodian national integrity had a dangerous immediacy.

The Geneva Conference

The decision to convene a conference on Indochina was made on February 17, 1954, during four-power talks on Berlin. The conference, which was also to consider the question of Korea, was scheduled to begin on April 26, but the plenary sessions on Indochina did not begin until May 8. Unfortunately for the Western powers, this proved to be an unhappy coincidence: The French fortress at Dien Bien Phu had fallen the day before. The participants in the conference were France, Britain, the United States, Communist China, the Soviet Union, and the three Associated States. The Viet-Minh was represented by delegates of the Democratic Republic of Viet-Nam. The military conflict had centered on control of Viet-Nam; Laos and Cambodia had been of a much lower order of priority. During the Geneva discussions, however, agreement on Laos and Cambodia was a greater obstacle to a successful settlement.

It became evident at the outset of the conference that a principal point of dispute would be the demands of the Communist representatives that the Cambodian Resistance Government be recognized and seated at the conference table. This position was most forcibly advocated by the Viet-Minh delegate, Pham Van Dong, who refused to recognize that the situations in Cambodia and Laos were different from that in Viet-Nam, where the French had admitted the existence of a state of civil war. Private discussions between the British Foreign Secretary, the Chinese Premier, and the Soviet Foreign Minister also failed to secure any agreement on this issue. Pham Van Dong insisted that the conference invite the representatives of the Khmer Resistance and Pathet Lao governments to participate in its work. The Cambodian delegation, however, refused to make the slightest concession to the Communist point of view. The head of the Cambodian delegation, Sam Sary, pointed out, "If there is a Free [sic] Government of Free Khmer we do not know of that government and I would submit that it has been created for a particular purpose." [27] He insisted that the Free Khmers were foreigners manipulated by a foreign bloc.

The participants in the conference agreed that separate armistices be concluded in each of the three associated states, but otherwise made no progress toward either a specific settlement on Cambodia or a more general agreement for Indochina. The British Foreign Secretary had based his hopes for success in the negotiations on being able to persuade the Chinese of the advantages of establishing what he described as a "protective pad" in Indochina, and of the disadvantages of possible American intervention should the conference fail to reach a settlement. He believed that the Chinese Government would welcome a respite from international tension after its exhausting intervention in Korea and would see the benefit of establishing buffer states behind which it could devote itself to socialist reconstruction.

On June 16, British Prime Minister Anthony Eden met privately with Chinese Premier Chou En-lai, and for the first time during the conference there appeared a genuine prospect of agreement. Chou En-lai informed Eden that he thought he could persuade the Viet-Minh to withdraw from Cambodia and Laos. China, he said, would recognize their royal governments if there were no American bases in the territories.[28] The following day, prospects brightened even further when the participants in the conference agreed on proposals to enable representatives of the Cambodian and Viet-Minh military commands to begin negotiations on the cessation of hostilities in Cambodia. Acceptance of direct talks between the Cambodians and the Viet-Minh made it apparent that the question of the existence of an alternative Cambodian government had ceased to be an obstacle to a final settlement. The conference adjourned while the parties concerned discussed the cease-fire provisions.

The final stage of the Geneva discussions began on July 12 and lasted little more than a week. It soon became apparent that Chou En-lai was sympathetic to Eden's concept of a general settlement. He was quite insistent, however, when they met on July 17, that Cambodia and the other states of Indochina were to be independent, sovereign, and neutral. As neutral states, they should definitely not, he felt, participate in the proposed defense arrangements for Southeast Asia. Eden was able to assure him that, as far as he knew, none of the powers intended that the Associated States would become members of the proposed organization.[29]

The conference reached a final agreement for the three states of Indochina on July 21. In Cambodia's case, the agreement provided for a cease-fire and for the withdrawal of foreign armed forces and what were described as foreign military personnel. Khmer Resistance members who were natives of Cambodia were to be demobilized within thirty days; the Cambodian Army was not to take hostile action against them. The Cambodian Government committed itself to integrate all citizens, without discrimination, into the national community and affirmed that all Cambodian citizens could participate freely as electors and candidates in general elections by secret ballot.

Whatever satisfaction the Cambodian delegation felt at securing acceptance of the principle of Viet-Minh withdrawal and the recognition of one legitimate government, it still felt some anxiety about its external security. The basis of the private agreement between Chou En-lai and Eden was that a settlement should be based on neutralization of the Indochinese successor states. The Cambodian Government, however, refused to be restricted by the implications of neutralization. In the final hours of the conference, Cambodian representatives doggedly maintained their position on this issue until the other delegates became exhausted, and the Cambodians won their point. At 2:00 A.M. on the morning of July 21, the agreement on the cessation of hostilities was signed. This agreement included the declaration that: "The Royal Government of Cambodia will not join in any agreement with other states, if this agreement carries for Cambodia the obligation to enter into a military alliance not in conformity with the principles of the U. N. Charter, or, as long as its security is not threatened, the obligation to establish bases on Cambodian territory for the military forces of foreign powers." [30] By this declaration, the Cambodian Government clearly reserved the right to call for military assistance from abroad in the event of any recurrence of the Viet-Minh threat. Indeed, the terms of the declaration left sufficient freedom of movement for Cambodia to request membership in the Southeast Asian defense organization the United States was then sponsoring. At that time, before the Geneva settlement had demonstrated its efficacy, at least as far as Cambodia was concerned, there is reason to believe that Cambodia contemplated such membership.

At the conclusion of the Geneva Conference, Cambodian independence had received great power imprimatur and international recognition.[31] This free and independent state did not regard the future with blind optimism. Independence was not an unmixed blessing; with national fulfillment came sole responsibility to ward off hostile forces, which the government believed had withdrawn only temporarily.

3

Cambodia Chooses Neutrality

During the Geneva Conference, the Cambodian delegation appeared as resolutely anti-Communist as the representatives of the United States. The behavior of the Cambodian delegates in the closing hours of the conference was a clear demonstration of their government's determination to resist Communist blandishments. They, like the United States, had serious doubts about the efficacy of any accord reached at Geneva and so were in no way disposed to accept, without reservations, the role of a neutral buffer state that had been chosen for them in private negotiations between the Chinese Premier and the British Foreign Secretary. The Cambodians refused to be committed to eschew military alliances when they expected that within a year the Viet-Minh menace would reappear at their frontiers. The threat appeared to them as traditional Vietnamese imperialism in Communist guise.[1] To combat this threat there seemed little alternative to reliance on the United States. The French were in no mood to provide a guarantee; their days in Indochina were over. Besides, renewed military ties with France, the former colonial power, would certainly have dangerous internal repercussions and would corroborate Democrat and Issarak charges that the King had been in collusion with the French. The Cambodians had a clear order of priorities about national security, and it seemed that only aid from the United States could meet those requirements.[2]

Cambodia had at first sought an agreement for automatic American assistance in the event of renewed aggression against Cambodia,[3] but the United States had turned away from specific commitments that would involve deploying land forces in mainland Southeast Asia and was more inclined to see Cambodia as a member of the proposed security system for Southeast Asia. In the circumstances, Cambodia had no alternative but to be persuaded that the broader arrangement the United States envisaged would provide for Cambodia's security needs.[4] Cambodia, however, was not to participate in the meeting at Manila in early September that inaugurated the Southeast Asia Treaty Organization (SEATO). The agreement between Chou En-lai and Anthony Eden, to which French Premier Pierre Mendès-France was also a party, prevented the postcolonial governments of Indochina from attending. The United States would have preferred to see these states represented at Manila, but was obliged to respect the commitment of its allies, whom it considered even more essential to associate with the defense system for Southeast Asia. Dulles was later to explain that "the Indo-China situation was considered by some of the treaty signatories as creating obstacles to these three countries (Cambodia, Laos, and South Viet-Nam) becoming actual parties to the treaty at the present time." [5]

The Southeast Asia Collective Defense Treaty—officially establishing SEATO—was signed in Manila on September 8, 1954. The signatory states were Britain, France, the United States, Australia, New Zealand, Thailand, Pakistan, and the Philippines. The purpose of the organization was to underwrite militarily the Geneva Agreements on Indochina. The members of SEATO decided to incur specific obligations toward the three non-Communist states of Indochina—without demanding anything from them in return. In a protocol attached to the treaty, Cambodia, Laos, and South Viet-Nam were designated as states to which Article Four (providing for collective measures in the event of armed attack) could apply. Action under this article would take place only at the invitation or with the consent of the governments named in the protocol.

The "Mantle of Protection," to use Dulles' phrase about the protocol arrangement, did not imply the type of commitment the Cambodian Government had requested initially. When reporting on the Manila Conference to President Eisenhower, Dulles made it abundantly clear that the treaty would require no material changes in the military planning of the United States, which maintained at all times "powerful naval and air forces in the Western Pacific capable of striking at any aggressor by means and at places of our choosing." [6] The experience of the crisis in Indochina had dissuaded Dulles from a military infrastructure for SEATO similar to that of the North Atlantic Treaty Organization (NATO). Despite pressure from Thailand and Australia, Dulles was not eager to dispatch American ground troops specifically to the treaty area. He had already faced American military opposition to committing troops to the inhospitable terrain of Indochina. In the Pentagon, there was then a clear aversion to deploying troops in circumstances less favorable than in Korea, where an inconclusive stalemate had turned opinion against similar ventures. An additional consideration was the existing strain on American military resources throughout the world. Dulles wrote, ". . . the responsibilities of the United States are so vast and far flung that we believe we would serve best not by earmarking forces for particular areas in the Far East but by the deterrent of mobile striking power plus strategically placed reserves." [7] Dulles was aware of the restraining influence exercised by the Chinese over the North Vietnamese at·Geneva. He most probably envisaged any aggression in terms of a Communist Chinese directive and accordingly believed that the ability to pose a nuclear threat to the Chinese mainland would provide the most efficacious deterrent to renewed conflict in mainland Southeast Asia.

For Cambodia, the protocol arrangement gave rights without duties, it offered formal protection without ideological commitment. Any concern over Allied disunity and the unwillingness of the United States to establish its physical presence in Indochina was in part compensated by the threat to any prospective aggressor of the SEATO offer.[8] At the time, the most likely prospect for aggression came still from the Communists; difficulties with non-Communist neighbors had not yet arisen.

The unilateral form of the offer—involving no corresponding obligation on the part of Cambodia—proved to be most fortunate. Because they had no direct obligations, the beneficiaries of the protocol arrangement did not automatically antagonize the Chinese Government, which understood the Geneva Agreements to mean that the Americans would not establish their physical presence within the Indochina successor states. The protocol arrangement was based on the absence of American military presence. Cambodia was able to deny any association with SEATO and even to renounce its rights, without, of course, removing the ubiquitous American presence from the area. It was thus possible to avoid provoking the Communists, who were capable of posing a threat to Cambodia of a kind that SEATO, it was later demonstrated, was incapable of meeting. The form of the SEATO commitment to the protocol states brought a measure of protection against a threat of a certain kind, i.e., open aggression, but left Cambodia sufficient freedom of maneuver to determine a pattern of international relationships that could provide against threats of a different nature.

The implementation of the Geneva Accords improved Cambodia's security position both internally and externally and alleviated the desperate need for a military guarantee that had existed in May, 1954. Although Viet-Nam was divided at the 17th Parallel, and in Laos the insurgent Pathet Lao gained a substantial territorial foothold in the northern provinces of Phong Saly and Sam Neua, Cambodia emerged from Geneva politically undivided. The royal government won full control over the whole area of the former French protectorate, and the Viet-Minh speedily withdrew its forces, even before the International Control Commission began to function.[9] By October, 1954, the Viet-Minh threat to Cambodia had begun to recede visibly, and most rebel Issaraks had left their

forest retreats to receive certificates empowering them to participate in forthcoming elections.

The effective implementation of the Geneva Accords was a
more significant factor than the unilateral guarantee from SEATO
in removing the immediate threat to Cambodia's territorial integrity. Sihanouk was certainly aware of the growing influence and
power of the Chinese People's Republic, and the Cambodian delegates to the Geneva Conference must have reported to him on the
degree of influence that the Chinese Premier had appeared to
exercise over the representatives of the Viet-Minh. China's willingness to sponsor a settlement that provided for only limited
Communist gains and, in the case of Cambodia, none at all, attracted his interest. The possible recurrence of Viet-Minh activity
was a constant anxiety, particularly as it could appear in the subversive form for which the SEATO guarantee need not provide
adequately. On the other hand, any commitment of foreign troops
to Cambodian soil would bring additional problems. This realiza-
tion was brought home in February, 1955, when there were public
protests during Dulles' visit to Phnom Penh to discuss American
military aid to Cambodia. Sihanouk's difficulties, both external and
internal, were such that solution to one problem could well aggravate another. He had obtained a guarantee against open aggression, but there was increasing doubt as to whether an external
threat would again present itself openly. At least the guarantee
involved no reciprocal obligations and could be explained away
so as not to alarm neighboring states or antagonize internal opponents. There remained, however, the problem of providing for effective security against an externally directed internal threat, and
in this Sihanouk had to try to avoid antagonizing domestic opponents by undue association with the so-called imperialist countries
or offending a country like China, which had demonstrated its
ability to restrain Cambodia's external enemies.

The Indian Government showed Sihanouk the way out of his
dilemma. India was then seeking to secure the peace of Asia and
her own interests by establishing the peaceful intent of China.

Following a visit by Indian Prime Minister Nehru in November, 1954, Sihanouk began to see that, by following the example of India's neutral way, he could avoid incurring the displeasure of Communist China. Sihanouk was encouraged in this neutral direction by members of Nehru's diplomatic entourage who "did not fail to expound the theory that the Indian sphere of influence which Red China would have to respect coincided with the borders of Indian cultural influence. It was obvious that this sphere of influence included both Laos and Cambodia, but not Viet-Nam." [10] Sihanouk seemed particularly receptive to the notion of a league of peaceful states committed to neither bloc. In December, Cambodian Prime Minister Penn Nouth indicated his country's neutral posture between East and West. He pointed out that while aid from the West would be welcomed, its acceptance would not be allowed to compromise his country's freedom of action. In March, 1955, Sihanouk visited Prime Minister Nehru in New Delhi. A joint communiqué issued on this occasion expressed Sihanouk's appreciation of India's approach to world problems and India's willingness to assist Cambodia in whatever ways it could. [11]

The meetings with Nehru appeared to be a major influence on Sihanouk's political thinking. Until the latter part of 1953, he had been regarded as a willing tool of the French and certainly not as a fitting associate of Nehru, the prestigious architect of nonalignment. At a time when Cambodia had barely achieved its independence and international recognition, receiving attention from the Indian Prime Minister must have been flattering. Sihanouk commented a year later, "Since he [Nehru] expounded a few principles in international relations which were bearing fruit in lessening international tension I have been following them." [12]

Although the Cambodian Government had formally committed itself to neutralism, it still entertained certain anxieties about that policy. Cambodia's response to India's overtures was undoubtedly an attempt to find further cover against the predatory intent of the Viet-Minh. The Cambodian Government was alarmed by the Chinese attempt to sponsor, together with the North Vietnamese,

the Khmer Resistance Government. While later Chinese concessions indicated a change in this position, Cambodia remained wary
of the influence of the Chinese People's Republic. In March, 1955,
the Cambodian Government began discussions with the United
States on the provision of military assistance, but before these negotiations were successfully concluded, the Bandung Conference
gave Sihanouk the opportunity to obtain the Communist assurances he so desperately needed.

The Bandung Conference

The conference of Asian and African countries held at Bandung,
Indonesia, in April, 1955, was essentially an attempt to demonstrate Afro-Asian solidarity. It was by no means a forum for fellow
spirits, and distrust of Communism was as prevalent among the
members as were tirades against colonialism. For Communist
China and North Viet-Nam, the Bandung Conference was an opportunity to establish their credentials as peaceful nations. For
Cambodia, it was an opportunity to test those declarations of
peaceful intent.

Sihanouk went to Bandung favorably disposed to the practice
of neutralism, but still somewhat concerned about his Communist
neighbors. His public statements made this abundantly clear. He
said that Cambodia was independent and neutral, and, having
adopted this position, had "the dangerous privilege of standing
the test and application of *Pancha Shila*" (the five principles of
peaceful coexistence). He continued, "It will be the test of the
more powerful nations to set the example, to give proofs and guarantees to smaller nations." [13] On other occasions, he boldly announced that the practicability of coexistence would depend on
the Communists; it would be up to them to reassure the rest of
the world of their peaceful intentions. Chou En-lai, as the head
of the Chinese Communist delegation to the conference, was sufficiently concerned by these pronouncements of distrust to invite

Sihanouk to lunch together with the head of the North Vietnamese delegation. China and North Viet-Nam assured Sihanouk that they would adhere faithfully to the *Pancha Shila* with Cambodia. Chou's assurances seem to have impressed Sihanouk; his subsequent behavior certainly suggests that Bandung marked a turning point for him.

Chou En-lai was apparently just as keen to seek assurances from Sihanouk of Cambodia's neutrality. His evident keenness for Cambodia to eschew any American involvement probably impressed the Cambodian leader more than his straightforward declaration of peaceful intent.[14] Sihanouk was now willing to accept the Chinese stipulation if it did not preclude a provision for limited American assistance. He willingly exchanged assurances with Chou En-lai, particularly on association with SEATO. The following year, Sihanouk told a newspaper correspondent, "During the Bandung Conference, Mr. Chou En-lai asked me during a long discussion what was this military agreement which bound us to the U.S.A. I was able to show him that we had not signed any pact of this kind and it was not Cambodia which had asked for the protection of SEATO." [15] The SEATO protocol was serving Cambodia well—it could be disavowed, yet it served a protective purpose. As SEATO had promised its protection gratuitously, with no corresponding obligations, there was no reason to accept such an offer publicly until China and North Viet-Nam had actually demonstrated hostility. As long as the Chinese appeared friendly, there was no point in identifying with a military alliance that was a direct challenge to China. Indeed, to seek shelter beneath such a protective arm in a non-crisis situation could well invoke the very hostility Cambodia was so keen to avoid.

Sihanouk had thus achieved a position of carefully balanced nonalignment. On the one hand, he had a gratuitous offer of protection, which was sufficient to alarm the Chinese over the prospect of American bases in Cambodia. From the Communists, who needed time for internal consolidation and development, he had received assurances dependent on his commitment to neutrality. This commitment, however, did not preclude the acceptance of a minimal level of American military assistance, which fitted the American desire for a military undertaking to Cambodia. The United States was prepared to provide for the needs of Cambodia's small army as well as to continue its economic assistance. The Cambodian Government was happy to receive assistance in a form that the Chinese could not construe as establishing an American physical presence in Cambodia.

In May, 1955, the United States and Cambodia signed an aid agreement providing for thirty American officers to go to Cambodia to estimate the needs of the Royal Army and then to assist in the use of equipment it would supply. On signing the agreement, the Cambodian Government made it plain that it had not entered into a military alliance and that the United States would not acquire bases in Cambodia. It also informed the International Supervisory and Control Commission for Cambodia that the agreement in no way constituted a military alliance and that Cambodia would scrupulously respect the terms of the Geneva Agreements.[16]

Although the Chinese press criticized the military aid agreement as a gross violation of the Geneva Agreements,[17] Cambodia itself received only a moderate reprimand; it was pictured as an innocent duped by the evil machinations of the United States rather than as a willing partner. This indicated that the arrangement was not intolerable to Peking, which left the job of direct protest to North Viet-Nam. Only two months after the signing of the aid agreement, Sihanouk claimed that Chou En-lai had informed him at their Bandung meeting that "China recognized Cambodia's right to organize her internal defences and get foreign military instructors." [18] This would seem to confirm that Communist China was not too alarmed by the agreement (it was certainly no threat to China) and had received satisfactory assurances that United States military aid would not involve United States military presence within Cambodia.

The Domestic Roots of Neutrality

Cambodia's increasing insistence that it would remain neutral in the Cold War was not solely the result of external circumstances. Sihanouk was aware of the domestic difficulties he was likely to face after Cambodia attained its independence. The rather spectacular and dramatic process by which the French had been persuaded to concede Cambodian independence had attracted considerable popular support to the throne and forestalled, for the time being, the clashes between King and Assembly that had been a common feature of pre-independence politics, but opposition to the King within the Democratic Party and among the Issaraks had not melted overnight. The difficulties he experienced after his return to Phnom Penh in November, 1953, pointed to an unresolved problem.

Under the Geneva Accords, the Cambodian Government had promised to integrate all citizens, without discrimination, into the national community and to guarantee their constitutional rights. It had also promised to hold general elections. The prospect of elections, in which Issaraks and their allies in the Democratic Party could participate without restraint, foreshadowed a return to the earlier situation, but with the likely differences that the Assembly would prove more vigorous and that the throne would rule less and reign more. The King's attitude to Son Ngoc Thanh indicated his apprehension. Thanh had somewhat foolishly delayed his return to Phnom Penh from the Northwest until after the conclusion of the Geneva Conference. He then sought to benefit from its provisions of amnesty and, in November, sent a message to the King apologizing for his lack of judgment, professing his loyalty, and requesting an audience. Unfortunately for Thanh, his approaches to the King were in private and did not become public knowledge until some time later. It has been suggested that if he had first proceeded to establish himself in Phnom Penh under the protection of the International Control Commission he may well have succeeded in re-entering public life.[19] The King, however, was not able to summon up trust in the man because of his previous record and was not eager to see Thanh repeat the triumphal entry he had made into the capital in November, 1951, on his return from exile in France. Sihanouk was absolutely determined not to permit Thanh or his close supporters any role in Cambodian politics. The King refused Thanh's request for an audience, and had him publicly denounced as a traitor and as one who had sought to obstruct the efforts to achieve independence. By forcing Thanh once more into exile, the King had merely dealt with a partially discredited opponent; he had by no means succeeded in restructuring his country's political process to ensure the supremacy of the throne or the necessary harmony of public life.

It eventually became evident to Sihanouk that he would be forced to take some sort of political initiative to prevent a recurrence of Democratic Party dominance. The referendum held on February 7, 1955—which Sihanouk had promised the people in June, 1952—had increased his confidence. The people were asked to vote on whether the royal mission had been satisfactorily fulfilled, and the result was overwhelmingly in Sihanouk's favor.

After this satisfying demonstration of support, the King turned to the question of normalizing political life. He first set up an interim government to prepare for elections on April 17, which would be supervised by the International Control Commission. At the time, there seemed no prospect of a real electoral contest. The Democratic Party was the most widely supported party and had a reputation for active demands for independence and constant opposition to French rule. There was no reason to expect that they would not form the next government.

Attempts to forestall this prospect began soon after the result of the referendum had been declared. Petitions began to arrive at the Royal Palace urging the postponement and even cancellation of elections. Provincial delegations met with the King and urged that he retain control of the machinery of government. Sihanouk responded with a pledge that he would ensure that elections would be held only after the electoral system had been revised. Although the spontaneous character of these demonstrations is certainly suspect, they were not necessarily organized with the knowledge of the King. But given the reverence with which the incumbent of the Cambodian throne is traditionally treated, Sihanouk would have had no difficulty in interpreting the demands for a cancellation of elections as representing the true interests of his people.

On February 19, the King summoned the diplomatic corps and the representatives of the International Control Commission to the Palace to tell them about a series of proposed constitutional changes to establish a democracy that the people would understand. These changes, if acted upon, would also remedy his somewhat handicapped political position. Claiming that he was impelled by popular demand, Sihanouk sought to eliminate the political party system. In its place, he suggested a process of indirect elections on an individual nonparty basis to an assembly that would be powerless to remove governments. Under this system, cabinets would be appointed by and directly responsible to the King. Sihanouk sought also to introduce a system of residence qualifications that would automatically exclude the candidacy of returned Issaraks. Finally, the King advocated that elections be postponed and that a referendum be held on his constitutional proposals. After the result of the referendum had become known, elections could be held. These measures would have emasculated the Democratic Party and prevented the re-establishment of an alternative locus of power to the King. It is difficult to assess whether the King expected these proposals to pass unopposed, especially the provisions that appeared to contravene those parts of the Geneva Agreements that applied to Cambodia.

The members of the International Control Commission were undoubtedly disturbed by the prospect that the proposals might be incompatible with the Geneva Agreements, but the Commission did not take an official stand on the matter and it never received an authorized version of the proposals. Individual members of the

Commission, however, sought to persuade the King against going ahead with his constitutional initiative.[20] The King was also subject to pressure from his Democratic Party opponents, who sought to exploit the issue to discredit him. On February 28, Premier Leng Ngeth informed the members of the Commission that elections would be held, after all, on the basis of the 1947 Constitution.

On March 2, the King dramatically altered the political situation by announcing that he intended to abdicate the throne in favor of his father, Prince Norodom Suramarit. Sihanouk informed his subjects in a broadcast that if he stayed on the throne he would no longer be able to satisfy their interests.[21] Clearly, he recognized that his political role would be limited if he continued as King within the bounds of the 1947 Constitution. A return to party politics would relegate him to the position of a figurehead, which he was not prepared to tolerate. He decided, therefore, to break the formal fetters of kingship in order to deal freely with his political opponents, but not on equal terms; he would enter the political arena carrying an aura of majesty that would be a substantial advantage against his opponents. To be king in Cambodia is to be no ordinary mortal. The man who stepped down from the throne in favor of his father retained those godlike qualities that are an integral part of kingship in Cambodia, and he exploited them to political effect.

Abdication was, for the King, the only way to obstruct the return of the Democrats to dominance in public life. As an alternative focus for public support, he established the Sangkum Reastre Niyum, which was more of a *rassemblement* than a real political party. It was a mass organization cutting across old party lines and based on loyalty to the nation and to Sihanouk (the two were considered to be coincident). Sangkum was represented as the means of achieving a necessary unity that had been compromised by the proliferation of political parties. With the announcement of the formation of this mass organization, many of the smaller political groupings that had little prospect of electoral success dissolved themselves and became attached to Sangkum. There were also some significant resignations from the Democratic Party, but this body was not willing to eschew the prospects of a return to power. Because the regime backed Sangkum, the civil servants undoubtedly saw personal advantage in supporting it and did so almost unanimously; they were able to generate great support for Sangkum in the provinces.[22]

After the formation of Sangkum, polling was postponed until September 11, and the election campaign began in earnest. Opposition to Sangkum came principally from the Democratic Party and, to a lesser extent, from a new association, the Pracheachon (People's) Party, which was believed to be Communist inspired [23] and which drew its main support from returned Issaraks of leftist persuasion. While Sangkum sought to capitalize on Sihanouk's success in obtaining complete independence, the principal opposition groups tried to discredit Sangkum by suggesting that Sihanouk was substituting American for French influence and by warning against the prospect of American economic domination. Their claims were more or less substantiated by the agreement in May, 1955, whereby the United States would provide economic and military assistance to Cambodia. Agitation on this issue must have demonstrated the need for Sihanouk to leave no doubt as to Cambodia's independence. He sought to shift attention from the immediate question of the aid agreement by promising to present the question of foreign aid for public discussion and approval at a later date. Indeed, Sihanouk disclaimed all knowledge of the negotiations that preceded the agreement and sought to blame the provisional government.

Sangkum enjoyed special electioneering advantages during the campaign. It was effectively supported by the Ministries of Information and Interior and had a monopoly of the national radio. Sangkum's opponents were subject to constant harassment. They often found themselves in difficulty over a very loose interpretation of the crime of *lèse-majesté*. At the outset of the campaign, the Pracheachon was refused permission to register to participate in the elections on the ground that it was an international association. The authorities relented only after the International Control Commission intervened to suggest that the banning of the Pracheachon could invalidate the elections.[24] Later in the campaign, the Commission reported instances of Democratic Party meetings broken up by supporters of Sangkum while police stood by, making no effort to intervene.

When the elections finally took place, the Control Commission concluded that polling was conducted in a very correct manner. By this time, the victory of Sangkum was probably so assured that the electoral process could be permitted to proceed unhindered. The elections resulted in an overwhelming victory for Sihanouk, whose party polled 83 per cent of the actual vote and consequently captured all the seats in the National Assembly. Sangkum had achieved success by gaining almost solid support in the rural areas, where it had capitalized on its electoral symbol—a picture of Norodom Sihanouk. To the peasants, the formal abdication of their revered monarch had not altered his venerated position. The Control Commission remarked, "The entrance of Prince Sihanouk into public life transformed the national scene and served as a major factor in the overwhelming victory of the Popular Socialist Community." [25]

Although he was generally satisfied with the outcome of the elections, Sihanouk nevertheless entertained certain doubts. In twenty-five of the ninety-one constituencies, opposition candidates had received at least 25 per cent of the vote recorded by Sangkum while in six they had received approximately 50 per cent.[26] To Sihanouk, these figures indicated that there was still a hard core opposed to his authority and that he would have to act cautiously to avoid providing this opposition with opportunities to enhance its political position.

A Demonstration of Neutrality

Sihanouk's experience at the hands of the domestic opposition made it necessary to demonstrate that Cambodia's newly won independence was genuine. The one charge that could undermine his re-established position of eminence was that of appearing to compromise his country's independence. A neutral stand in the Cold War would thus disarm those who sought to encourage dissidence at the expense of the throne.

The neutralist policy Sihanouk adopted had decided advantages. Although it reactivated traditional antagonisms with Cambodia's neighbors, threats from these countries consolidated national unity more than anything else had. At the same time, he could exploit the Cold War to national advantage by establishing good relations with the enemies of Thailand and South Viet-Nam, both firm adherents of the anti-Communist cause. This policy eventually embittered relations with the United States, but this, in turn, robbed the Cambodian left of an effective voice. Public denunciations of the United States were never carried to the stage where that government thought it necessary to halt its aid program to Cambodia. The United States could tolerate Sihanouk's strictures as long as Cambodian neutrality was not a guise for *de facto* membership in the Communist camp. When U.S. aid was discontinued in 1963, it was because Cambodia requested its termination.

At a news conference on the morrow of Sangkum's electoral triumph, Sihanouk reconfirmed Cambodia's course in foreign policy. His country would be committed to a neutral role and would neither join any defensive organization nor accept the gratuitous protection offered by SEATO. "We are neutralist," he declared. "We will fight Communists only if they attack us." [27] This statement did not foreshadow any softening of his earlier resolve to resist possible Communist threats. When, as Prime Minister, Sihanouk presented his newly formed cabinet to the National Assembly at the beginning of October, he pointed out that charges that Cambodia's acceptance of American military aid was compromising its independence were baseless. He also stressed the continuing menace of the Communists allegedly operating in the eastern provinces, charging that they wished to enslave the Khmer State to the yoke of the Annamite Viet-Minh State.

Sihanouk had agreed to accept the office of Prime Minister for a brief term of three months, hoping that this would be a sufficient period to create a stable government. After his resignation in January, 1956, to go on holiday in France, it became evident that the Cambodian political process had still to undergo fundamental change. While the pre-independence struggle between Assembly and throne had ceased, political life was still marked by petty squabbles and undue striving for personal advantage. Sangkum had yet to overcome the factional tendencies engendered by its varied composition. The President of the National Assembly was appointed Prime Minister to replace Sihanouk, but was forced to resign only three days after his inauguration as a result of popular demonstrations urging the ex-King's return as Prime Minister. However these demonstrations may have originated, their effect was to point to Sihanouk's apparently indispensable role. The members of the Assembly were totally unable to agree on a government that was not headed by Sihanouk. The crisis was resolved only when he consented to resume office. By the end of March, however, Sihanouk had offered his resignation a second time. This departure from office was prompted by events external to Cambodia.

During January, Sihanouk visited a number of foreign countries. At the end of the month, he arrived in the Philippines. His appearance produced speculation in the Philippine press that Cambodia was likely to renounce its neutral foreign policy, if not to become a member of SEATO. There is little independent reliable evidence as to what ensued in Manila, but Sihanouk subsequently claimed that he was subjected to undue pressure inspired by the United States to make him alter the course of his country's foreign policy. One can be reasonably sure that Sihanouk's hosts—enthusiastic members of SEATO—were not sympathetic toward his neutralist views. They were not enamored of the speech he made before the Philippine Congress, in which he stated that Cambodia, although not attracted by Communism, was in no way threatened by Communist aggression and that his country would continue its current foreign policy as long as that was so. He stressed that he had no desire to be associated with hostile ventures against a

China that had shown only friendship toward Cambodia. He went on to assert that to join SEATO would provide the Communists with an excuse to intervene in Cambodia.[28] These were not acceptable views to his Filipino hosts, particularly as they found favor among the nationalist-neutralist grouping in Congress led by Senator Claro Recto. Despite his determined espousal of a point of view hardly acceptable to a SEATO member, there was no indication in the sensitive, if not always accurate, Philippine press that his visit had in any way been marred by friction or open disagreement with members of the host government. On Sihanouk's departure, President Magsaysay announced, "The Prince has a perfect right to advocate and follow the policy that is best for his country." [29]

While Sihanouk was in Manila, it became known that he intended to pay a visit to Peking in the near future. Shortly after his return to Phnom Penh, he left for China, arriving on February 13. In the Chinese capital, he was treated with great reverence and feted and acclaimed wherever he went. He was received with more deference than in the Philippines, and he could not help noticing the contrast between his receptions in the two capitals. Unlike many other visitors to China, he did not allow himself to marvel publicly at the achievements of the Communist regime, and he asserted on his return to Cambodia that such a regimented system would not suit the Cambodian people.

Sihanouk's views on foreign policy more than compensated for his skepticism on Chinese domestic achievements. He announced that Cambodia had rejected the automatic protection of SEATO, which he considered dishonorable. Sihanouk was not indulging in mere sycophantic pandering to the predelictions of his hosts, but was shrewdly eschewing an association that could lead to Communist subversion within Cambodia. His conversations with Chou En-lai had led him to believe that Cambodia could expect to avoid the attentions of its Communist neighbors as long as it could demonstrate that it was not a member or protective ward of the Westtern camp.

Sihanouk's rejection of SEATO's protection—which was not removed because of his public statements—resulted in the signing of the Sino-Cambodian Declaration of Friendship. This marked the beginning of an association that the Chinese, who had so many other priorities, were only too willing to encourage and indulge. As a mark of China's pleasure, Cambodia became the beneficiary of the first grant in aid ($22.4 million) by the Chinese People's Republic to a non-Communist country.[30]

On his return from Peking, Sihanouk found a dramatic deterioration in relations with Cambodia's neighbors Thailand and South Viet-Nam. Both of these countries had in the past ruled the territory that is now Cambodia, and their governments were somewhat disdainful of Cambodia's attempts to pursue a line different from their own. The visit to China no doubt changed an amused irritation to genuine alarm. All three countries had overseas Chinese communities (in Cambodia's case, 300,000) that they regarded with suspicion and mistrust. Thailand and South Viet-Nam regarded with considerable foreboding the association foreshadowed by the Sino-Cambodian Declaration of Friendship. Both nations had aligned themselves with the West in the Cold War. Thailand was a member of SEATO, and its capital city, Bangkok, was the headquarters of the organization. South Viet-Nam, like Cambodia, was covered by the SEATO protocol, but its involvement with the United States went far beyond that of Cambodia. United States financial backing had been instrumental in the initial consolidation of the Diem regime. Both countries regarded Sihanouk's visit as foolhardy and as an indication of his willingness to serve Chinese interests in Indochina.

South Viet-Nam and Thailand indicated their displeasure by closing their frontiers with Cambodia and imposing a virtual economic blockade. This was most serious in the case of the border with South Viet-Nam, because the Mekong and the port of Saigon were Cambodia's main channels of trade and supply. Financed by France, work had begun on a new port in the south near Kompong Som, to be linked to the capital by an American-built highway, but Cambodia's dependence on Saigon was still almost total.

Even today, free traffic on the Mekong is vital to Cambodia, and threats to block the river are not received lightly in Phnom Penh.

The sanctions employed by Thailand and South Viet-Nam were not related entirely to Sihanouk's flirtation with China. The blockade must be seen as the culmination of a series of petty conflicts that were given a new dimension by the Peking visit. Before Sihanouk first resigned as prime minister, friction between Cambodia and its neighbors was evident. Frontier incidents tended to be magnified in Cambodia because of historic friction between Cambodia and its neighbors. For example, Sihanouk became alarmed in November, 1955, when Vietnamese soldiers landed on Cambodian islands in the Gulf of Siam and confiscated some fishing vessels. This led to a virtual newspaper war between the two countries, and Cambodia reasserted its right to Cochinchina, where there was a significant Khmer minority. This irredentist sentiment —expressed periodically by Cambodian governments ever since the colony of Cochinchina had been merged into the State of Viet-Nam in 1949—was regarded with annoyance by the Saigon regime. Other differences existed between the two nations over rights of navigation on the Mekong and the fact that Cambodia had given asylum to political refugees from South Viet-Nam.

Similar differences existed between Cambodia and Thailand, which claimed that Cambodians had been provoking border incidents. At the same time, Sihanouk claimed that Son Ngoc Thanh was engaged in subversive activities from a base in Thailand. The Thai Government was annoyed at Cambodia's refusal to permit flights over its territory during SEATO exercises in February, 1956. Cambodia, of course—resenting the attitude of the Thais—regarded such an exercise as a deliberate provocation. Another issue of more symbolic than substantial moment had been the Thai occupation in 1949 of a derelict Khmer Temple at Prah Vihar. This temple directly overlooked the region Thailand had been forced to restore to Cambodia in November, 1946. Following the border incidents, which coincided with Sihanouk's visit to China, the Thais strengthened their position on the temple site. In February,

1956, patrols exchanged shots over the disputed temple, but the Thais continued to occupy the temple. The Cambodians could do little to remove them because of the difficulty of access from their side.

Sihanouk is a very sensitive man and often sees insults where none exist. In this case, he felt, with some justification, that Thai occupation of a site that was part of the Khmer heritage was a symbolic demonstration of that country's belief that it should exercise hegemony over its smaller neighbor. Sihanouk also reacted strongly to the newspaper strictures against him in Thailand and South Viet-Nam. His attitude toward the press had probably crystalized when he made use of American newspapers to embarrass the French in his campaign for independence. It is likely that he overestimated the influence of the press and was inclined with some justification to believe that, in the case of Thailand and South Viet-Nam, the press merely reflected the feeling of the government. In addition, he saw American influence behind what he regarded as a plan deliberately designed to bring Cambodia to its knees and to bring its foreign policy into line with that of its neighbors and their Western mentor, the United States.

In many speeches after his return to Phnom Penh, Sihanouk made derisory comments about the quality of aid Cambodia received from the United States. An incident then occurred which confirmed Sihanouk's belief that Cambodia was the victim of an American-inspired campaign to change its foreign policy: The United States halted its aid program at the same time that Thailand and South Viet-Nam imposed their economic blockade on Cambodia. An American diplomat who has served in Cambodia has claimed that the stoppage took place after frauds were discovered in the implementation of the program. He insists that the Cambodian Government itself temporarily suspended the imports.[31] Sihanouk seized on this incident as evidence that his disparaging remarks about U.S. aid, as well as his recent visit to China, had prompted the American Government to mastermind an insidious scheme against his country. He hinted that he was being coerced into joining SEATO through economic blockades and secret plots.

The crisis abated somewhat when Sihanouk resigned as Prime Minister at the end of March. One of the perplexing factors in this whole affair, suggesting that the crisis was compounded of artificial as well as genuine factors, was Sihanouk's explanation of his resignation as being prompted by friction with senior civil servants over the use of American aid funds. His position during the crisis was not consistent; for example, at a news conference at the end of March, he asserted that he had not been invited to join SEATO, but that the Western powers did not want him to declare that Cambodia was outside the protection of the organization.

On April 19, U.S. Secretary of State Dulles sent a letter to the Cambodian Foreign Minister, Nong Kimny, emphatically denying that the United States had threatened to cut off economic aid to Cambodia or had compelled South Viet-Nam and Thailand to exert economic pressure to force Cambodia into SEATO.[32] The U.S. Ambassador had previously assured Cambodia's King Suramarit that the acceptance of American aid did not involve conditions prejudicial to Cambodia's neutrality and independence. These actions prompted Sihanouk to declare that he had overwhelming proof of a plot in Manila against Cambodian neutrality. He suggested that comments in the Philippine press at the time of his visit were sufficient indication of what his hosts had expected. Much more conclusive proof, he claimed, was that a member of his entourage during the visit to the Philippines had violated his hospitality by urging him to deliver a speech to mitigate the effects of his expression of neutralist sentiment before the Filipino Congress. The Cambodian leader linked this alleged attempt at coercion with the difficulties he had experienced after his return from China, and he went on to assert that his immediate neighbors—encouraged by the United States—were also seeking to force Cambodia into SEATO.

It is difficult to form a dispassionate view of this whole affair which, on Cambodia's part, was related to genuine fears of its traditional antagonists. There is reason to believe that if American pressure was exerted, it was applied in Bangkok and Saigon to Cambodia's advantage. Such approaches, however, merely confirmed for Sihanouk that the United States had the ability to manipulate the strings of the neighboring "puppet states." It is undeniable that Cambodia's economic life was temporarily disrupted, and this experience made clear to Sihanouk his exposed position between two countries that were more likely to attract the sympathy of the United States than was neutral Cambodia. In this context, Sihanouk saw a practical value in developing new associations, particularly with Communist countries, which could serve as countervailing powers against his predatory neighbors.

Cambodia's immediate crisis was resolved when the United States declared its good intentions. Thailand and South Viet-Nam subsequently reopened their borders with Cambodia and restored diplomatic contacts. Sihanouk was able to use the episode to his advantage domestically. It has been suggested that his policy of neutrality had domestic origins that coincided with external geopolitical realities. As long as Sihanouk was determined to remain as national leader, he could not afford to give the still active supporters of the Democrats or the pro-Communist Pracheachon any opportunity to undermine his position. He had to establish his preeminence as the stalwart defender of national interests against evil-minded foreigners. He was able to play that role to great effect in the conflict with Thailand and South Viet-Nam, in which the United States stood conspicuously in the background. Sihanouk's embarrassment over the American arms agreement has been mentioned previously; he attempted to discredit criticism of that action at the Second National Congress of Sangkum, in December, 1955. At this meeting, the Congress approved the acceptance of American military aid, but only if the Americans would agree to certain restrictions. In April, 1956, Sihanouk called a third Congress open also to non-members of Sangkum, and on this occasion he reaped the internal benefits of the recent crisis.

The Congress was the scene of a general debate on foreign policy, and it concluded with unanimous reaffirmation of support for neutrality and nonadherence to SEATO or any other military alliance. The Congress also agreed that Cambodia would accept economic aid from any quarter, on the condition that the donor respect Cambodia's neutrality. Sihanouk used the Congress to announce the aid agreement with China and the prospect of further assistance from other Communist countries. The attention to external threats generated wholesale support for a policy that had been identified with Sihanouk's leadership. Sihanouk was thus able to exploit the crisis to consolidate national unity and to rally support in the face of an external menace. One indication of the real purpose of the Congress came during a discussion on a motion by the Pracheachon Party—a party that Sihanouk regarded as a proxy for the North Vietnamese regime. The Pracheachon motion envisaged a coalition between Sangkum and the remaining parties to defend Cambodia's neutrality. The Congress rejected this proposition, pointing out that the position of Cambodia as a neutral state was clear enough and that it was inappropriate for an opposition party that had made offensive attacks against the President of Sangkum to propose a resolution designed to weaken the association.

Thus, by establishing his nationalist credentials in the face of traditional and allegedly new enemies, Sihanouk was able to discredit the only political group that was sufficiently organized to undermine his position and threaten the unity of the nation. By demonstrating that Cambodia was threatened by the forces of both the Western and the Communist camps, Sihanouk ensured that domestic divisions based on ideological attachments would be stunted before they could prove inimical to national consensus. Sihanouk would thus balance between East and West, seeking necessary adjustments in the dispensation of Cambodia's favors when it became apparent that the delicate equilibrium of neutrality was being disturbed.

4

The Practice of Neutrality

By 1956, Cambodia appeared to have solved the more urgent problems arising from internal dissidence. The pre-independence conflict between Assembly and throne had been resolved by Sihanouk's abdication and his continuing direct involvement in political life. The Democratic Party—which, in addition to representing the extralegal movements with which it was associated, had been the principal source of legal opposition—had been soundly defeated in the elections of September, 1955. The members of the new Assembly, drawn from the ranks of Sangkum, owed their position to Sihanouk. Domestic political conflict did not disappear but now became chiefly a nuisance. Its principal features were petty squabbling among factions and personalities, bickering over self-seeking, and frequent cabinet reshuffling.

With the establishment of the Sangkum Assembly, Cambodia's priorities had come full circle. The recession of the direct Viet-Minh threat, in the latter part of 1954, had focused attention on internal dissension and problems of national unity. After Sihanouk had consolidated authority, however, his attention returned to external problems—specifically, the difficulties with Thailand and the neighboring portion of Viet-Nam. The renewal of threats from traditional foes confirmed for Sihanouk the necessity of pursuing a nonaligned foreign policy and created a more favorable climate for domestic harmony. Indeed, the manner in which these conflicts were publicized suggests that the Cambodian Government was aware of their integrative function.

The initial decision to adopt neutrality was based on domestic imperatives and a fear of provoking renewed Communist intervention. At Geneva and at Bandung, the Chinese Government had expressed concern about the prospect of an American military presence in Cambodia. At Bandung, Chou En-lai had inquired about Cambodia's association with SEATO, indicating that the Communist attitude toward Cambodia would be dictated by the nature of its alignments. Since the Communists had offered to tolerate a neutral Cambodia, Sihanouk espoused a conciliatory neutralism, underpinned by possible recourse to the Manila Protocol.

At the same time, Sihanouk's efforts to establish neutrality aggravated traditional antagonisms with Cambodia's anti-Communist neighbors, one of which was a member of SEATO. He could not count on Western backing to meet any threats from this quarter; the United States had made clear in the Manila Protocol that its obligations were restricted to instances of Communist aggression. Although this statement was related directly to the prospect of conflict between Pakistan and India, it also represented official American thinking. At the time of the Manila Protocol, the reservation appeared to have little relevance to Cambodia's situation. The situation had changed, and Sihanouk had justifiable doubts about securing protection from the United States against its allies. It seemed to Sihanouk that he must seek other sources of countervailing power to meet renewed threats to security.

Sihanouk appeared to derive comfort from the maxim that an enemy of an enemy is likely to become a friend, at least in some circumstances. Thus, he initiated a policy of balance, whereby the forces of one camp in the Cold War would check the forces of the other. In April, 1956, Sihanouk enunciated his foreign policy as follows: ". . . the influence of the Communist block shall counterbalance the influence of the Western bloc. From henceforth we shall hold out one hand to the West and the other to the Communists at the same time as we desire support from the active friendship of the neutrals." [1] At the same time, he expected that the principals of the two camps would exercise a measure of restraint over their subordinate allies.

Cambodia's geographic location made it more likely that this expectation would be realized in the case of the Communists. [2] Cambodia did not share a border with a Communist country, and North Viet-Nam's priorities were internal consolidation and reunification of Viet-Nam. But Cambodia was face to face with Thailand and South Viet-Nam, and its more immediate external problems derived from these anti-Communist countries.

To demonstrate his neutral intentions and to make it clear to his subjects that their independence was genuine, [3] Sihanouk set out in mid-1956 to visit the Soviet Union, Poland, Czechoslovakia, Yugoslavia, Sweden, and Spain. His tour brought dividends in diplomatic exchanges and offers of economic and technical assistance. In Moscow, Warsaw, and Prague, Sihanouk's hosts encouraged his foreign policy, and he himself reiterated Cambodia's desire to be friends with all countries willing to respect its neutrality. The Soviet Union had no special interests in Cambodia, but was happy to encourage a loosening of Cambodian attachments to the West. The Soviet Government may have had misgivings about the perplexing figure of a former king who enjoyed a traditional relationship with his people but practised the new diplomacy of the Third World, but they were nonetheless sympathetically disposed to his objectives. Sihanouk, for his part, enjoyed the deferential treatment accorded him by his new international acquaintances, which enhanced his own status and that of his country.

It is interesting that Sihanouk made no attempt at that time to enter into diplomatic relations with Communist China or North Viet-Nam. He had committed himself publicly to eschew such ties until single governments ruled over both these divided countries. His reception in Peking in February, 1956, had opened up the prospect of soliciting at least Communist diplomatic support to counter possible threats from his neighbors. At that time, however, he may have regarded too close an association with the nearer Communist countries as more harmful than beneficial. Remembering the repercussions of his visit to China, Sihanouk may have thought it more politic to avoid giving further cause for offense. He probably felt that diplomatic relations with China should be held in reserve, as a later resort. Indeed, such seems to have been the case when Cambodia did enter into full diplomatic relations with Peking in July, 1958.

Sihanouk's policy of strict nonalignment was reinforced by the Fourth National Congress, held in Phnom Penh in January, 1957, which amended the Cambodian Constitution to define neutrality as "Non-commitment to a military alliance or ideological bloc." The Congress also agreed on the alternatives to be pursued if neutrality failed to provide for national security. If Cambodia became the victim of external aggression, it would reserve the right to self-defense or an appeal to the United Nations. If those measures proved ineffectual, Cambodia would appeal to a powerful friend.[4] Sihanouk reiterated these alternatives the following year, in a speech before the United Nations General Assembly. In 1960, he made an explicit statement as to what was involved in the third alternative. He said: "If Cambodia were the object of an attack by the Viet-Minh and the Chinese People's Republic it could demand the support of the Free World and the United States, and, if the attack came from Thailand or South Viet-Nam it is certain that it would demand the aid of the Communist bloc and in particular the Chinese People's Republic." [5] The references to the Free World and the United States would suggest that while Cambodia was willing to reject publicly the gratuitous offer of protection by SEATO (and to reap the internal and external benefits that such a rejection incurred), its government seemed more secure in the knowledge of SEATO's existence. On the other hand, the fact that Sihanouk was willing, after having established diplomatic relations with Communist China, publicly to countenance the prospect of its aggressive intent suggested not only that he desired a genuine neutral equilibrium for his country but also that such a position was made possible by the existing balance of external forces.

Sihanouk did not maintain this posture much longer; in the same year, the drift of events in Laos and in South Viet-Nam indicated that a new balance of forces was coming into existence. This new balance effectively undermined the value of the West as a countervailing power helping to sustain the independence of Cambodia. For the time being, at least, Cambodia viewed neutrality in terms of an equal balance between East and West that fitted the geopolitical needs of the moment. But Cambodia's more immediate difficulties arose from conflicts with adherents of only one ideological camp, namely Thailand and South Viet-Nam.

Cambodia's Neighbors

THAILAND

The independence of Cambodia and the removal of the formal protective presence of France re-established a situation that had not existed since before 1863, with the important exception of the period of Japanese dominance in Southeast Asia. The successful reassertion of Thai claims to Cambodia's northwestern provinces in 1941 had a profound impact on Cambodian-Thai relations, and its effect was not moderated by the restoration of these regions to Cambodia after World War II. The 1941 annexations suggested that if Cambodia ever found itself without an external source of protection, Thailand would not hesitate to extend its domain at Cambodia's expense. Cambodia had further cause to distrust the Thais, who were said to have ambitions for a greater Thai state encompassing the Theravada Buddhist lands of Laos and Cambodia.[6] The Khmer Issarak movement had been organized and encouraged from Bangkok. The movement was disbanded after Cambodia became independent, but its leading figure, former Prime Minister Son Ngoc Thanh, was never reconciled with Norodom Sihanouk, who was determined to prevent Thanh's re-entry into Cambodian political life. Thanh remained in hiding in the forests along the Thai border until Cambodian military operations forced him to seek refuge in Thailand. His intermittent presence in Thailand seemed to intensify differences between the two states. Another factor aggravating Cambodian-Thai relations was Sihanouk's personal bitterness at the hostility with which he had been received in 1953, when he had requested political asylum in Thailand.

The fact that they had adopted different positions in the Cold War further divided Cambodia and Thailand. Thailand and South Viet-Nam both felt that Cambodia's neutrality was an open invitation to Communist penetration, which could drive a subversive wedge between the members of the anti-Communist alliance in mainland Southeast Asia. They came to regard Cambodia as the willing tool of the Communists. It has been suggested that the change in government in Thailand in October, 1958, which consolidated Marshal Sarit Thanarat in power, was precipitated in part by the anxiety of the Thai military at the establishment of diplomatic relations between Cambodia and to Chinese People's Republic the previous July.[7]

The issue that crystallized differences between Thailand and Cambodia was a dispute over the ruins of the ancient Khmer temple of Prah Vihar. The dispute in itself can hardly be described as a matter of substance, but it was certainly symptomatic of the two countries' mutual suspicion. For Cambodia, the temple was a symbol of her independence and of her determination to resist Thai blandishments. To have backed down on this issue might have encouraged the Thais to renew their claims to the northwestern provinces. For the Thais, it probably indicated their patronizing view of Cambodia and their desire to impose their hegemony. The actual controversy began several years before Cambodia became independent. Thailand had stationed keepers at the temple site in February, 1949, and pointedly ignored French requests for their withdrawal. Cambodia sought to dispatch its own keepers to the temple site after gaining independence but, on discovering that Thai keepers were still there, the Cambodians withdrew. In February, 1954, the Cambodian Government sent a note to the Thai Government requesting information about the presence of the Thai keepers. The Thai Government merely acknowledged the note. The following month, Cambodia notified Thailand that it proposed to send in troops. It did not dispatch the troops, but in June sent another note, pointing out that, as it understood that Thai police were now occupying the site, it would withhold Khmer forces, so as not to aggravate the situation.[8] The second note also required the withdrawal of the Thai police, but the Thai Government did not reply.[9] Thailand reinforced its police detachment early in 1956, during the period of strained relations that followed Sihanouk's visit to China.

Cambodia raised the issue formally, in May, 1957, in the form of a complaint to the International Control Commission. Because of internal differences, however, the Commission did not feel competent to act on this information. Thailand did not respond until April, 1958, when it sent a note to the Cambodian Government pointing out that treaties with France defining the Cambodian frontier were no longer applicable, as they had been signed under pressure.

Negotiations followed later that year, but they were inconclusive and only impaired an already unhappy relationship. Sihanouk himself went to Bangkok in July, 1958, to open preliminary discussions. A week after his visit, on July 24, Cambodia announced *de jure* recognition of the Chinese People's Republic. The Thais saw this measure as an attempt to intimidate them prior to the beginning of the actual negotiations.[10] At the same time, they were alarmed at the increased prospect of Communist infiltration.[11] The Thai Government had no doubt that there was a close connection between Cambodia's attempts to secure Prah Vihar and the arrival of a Communist Chinese ambassador in Phnom Penh. It reacted by declaring a state of emergency along the Cambodian border.

Despite these problems, negotiations between Thai and Cambodian representatives began as planned in August, but in an atmosphere hardly conducive to a settlement. The talks came to an abrupt end during the first week of September, when the parties were unable to agree on the terms of reference for a proposed mixed commission to mark their common boundary. The Cambodian delegation insisted that the proposed commission base its findings on the Franco-Thai Treaties of 1904 and 1907 and also on "documents annexed" (to the 1907 treaty), which included a map showing the temple on the Cambodian side of the frontier. The Thais objected to the inclusion of this map, claiming it was erroneous because the temple was actually situated physically on the Thai side of the watershed. The breakdown in negotiations was followed by strongly worded criticisms of Cambodia in the Thai press, and a violent demonstration was mounted outside the Cambodian Embassy in Bangkok.

The next initiative came from Cambodia, whose ambassador presented a note to Bangkok on November 24, requesting "a temporary *de facto* suspension" of diplomatic relations. The Thais retaliated by withdrawing their ambassador from Phnom Penh, closing the frontier, and suspending air service. The Cambodian Government announced that it intended to close its embassy in Bangkok, since relations with Thailand had become pointless. At this point, the Cambodians seemed inclined to arrest the drift of events, and they issued a statement to the effect that they were prepared to maintain a *chargé d'affaires* in Bangkok if Thailand reciprocated. The Thai Government then demanded—as a precondition to a resumption of relations—the release of thirty-two of its nationals, allegedly kidnapped by Cambodian forces. The Cambodian Government responded with counterclaims of a similar nature, but at the same time informed the Secretary-General of the United Nations that Thai troop concentrations along the frontier represented a threat to peace. Differences were settled and tempers calmed through the mediation of Baron Beck-Friis, a personal envoy of the Secretary-General. In January, 1959, the two nations exchanged prisoners and, on February 6, announced that their respective ambassadors would return to their posts.

The two neighboring countries did not, however, achieve a real reconciliation; recurrent incidents lent substance to their mutual suspicions. In Cambodia's case, evidence came to hand that Thailand had been interfering in its internal affairs. During January and February, 1959, while Baron Beck-Friis was still engaged in mediation, Cambodia announced that the Thai Government had been involved in two related plots designed to overthrow Sihanouk. These conspiracies involved disaffected supporters of Sihanouk, in particular the former Ambassador to London, Sam Sary. The guiding spirit behind this action, Sihanouk alleged, was the United States Central Intelligence Agency.[12]

Events associated with these plots were sufficient to convince the Cambodian Government that Thailand (and South Viet-Nam, equally implicated) was actively engaged in seeking to subvert the state. At the same time, the involvement of the CIA was proof enough that Cambodia's neighbors were being encouraged and abetted in their devilish schemes by their political mentor, the United States. It was too much to expect that Sihanouk should make the fine distinction between the CIA and the State Department. Indeed, he was to implicate a member of the United States Embassy in Phnom Penh.[13]

In spite of the allegations concerning the plot, the two nations made one further attempt to normalize relations. In June, 1959, at the end of the Thai Foreign Minister's visit to Phnom Penh, the two governments issued a joint communiqué committing themselves to avoid interference in each other's internal affairs and to prohibit activities harmful to each other's security. This *rapprochement* lasted only until Cambodia took the temple dispute to the International Court of Justice in October. Thailand immediately registered its displeasure[14] and sought to challenge the competence of the tribunal. In May, 1961, rejecting Thailand's petition, the Court ruled that it was competent to consider the case. From this time on, Thai-Cambodian relations deteriorated progressively.

In October, 1961, Sihanouk visited Tokyo after attending the Sixteenth Session of the United Nations General Assembly. During his stay in Tokyo, he gave a public lecture intended to explain Cambodian policy. The Thai Prime Minister took strong exception to remarks allegedly uttered in the course of this address. The Thais claimed Sihanouk had asserted that Cambodia would not fight so much against Communists as against pro-Western neighboring countries.[15] During the course of an official reception in Bangkok in October, 1961, attended by the diplomatic corps, Thai Prime Minister Sarit Thanarat had complained of the "annoying accusations and arrogance of a head of state who has constantly made himself known as an enemy of Thailand." Sarit went on to accuse this unspecified head of state of permitting his country to be used as a bridgehead to induce the Communists to harm neighboring countries. He concluded by suggesting that Thailand had to exercise restraint and to endure such annoyance "by taking consolation in the old proverbial tale of a pig challenging a lion to a fight."[16]

Sarit's remarks moved the Thai-Cambodian conflict to a new plane. Sihanouk construed the allusion to a pig as a personal insult as well as a reflection of disdain for a country whose international pretensions contrasted with its former vassal status. An indication of the bitter feeling Sarit's statement aroused was Sihanouk's decision to proclaim a national holiday to celebrate the death of the Thai Prime Minister in December, 1963.

The Cambodian Government reacted to the insult to its head of state by breaking off diplomatic relations with Thailand [17] on October 23, 1961, and putting its army in a state of alert. The Thai Government responded by closing the frontier. After this, acrimony and invective became the most common forms of communication between the two countries. The Thais reiterated charges about Cambodia's Communist associations, and the Cambodians repeated their claims of Thai expansionism.[18] Because of Thailand's affiliations with the United States, Cambodia was unable to dissociate the United States from its difficulties with Thailand. Sihanouk became increasingly convinced that the American Government was unwilling rather than unable to restrain its ally in its hostile endeavors. Indeed, he believed that common ideological sentiments motivated the United States to encourage rather than to restrain the Thais. Following the Cambodian-Thai diplomatic break of October, 1961, the Cambodian press indulged in bitter comment about the role of the United States.[19]

The severance of diplomatic relations between Cambodia and Thailand did not prevent the International Court of Justice from proceeding with the temple dispute. The case was decided in Cambodia's favor in June, 1962, and, after initial hesitation, the Thai Government complied with the ruling and evacuated the temple site.[20] Naturally, Prince Sihanouk treated the outcome of the case as a vindication of his personal involvement in the dispute and as a national triumph. The Thais, for their part, were as disappointed as the Cambodians were delighted. They were especially aggrieved at the presence before the Court, on Cambodia's behalf, of former U.S. Secretary of State Dean Acheson. Indeed, Acheson's pleading helped to win the day for Cambodia. Thailand accepted the Court's decision with some ill grace, and the judicial defeat exacerbated relations.

After the resolution of the temple dispute, relations moderated to a muted hostility, interrupted periodically by incidents, charges, and countercharges of a symptomatic nature. The death in December, 1963, of Marshal Sarit removed an element of personal antagonism from the relationship. His successor as Prime Minister, Thanom Kittikachorn, was not given to the type of abuse that so infuriates Sihanouk. Nevertheless, there was no indication that the two parties were willing to consider restoring diplomatic contact, despite continued United Nations mediation. Cambodian suspicions of Thai intentions were intensified after a temporary reoccupation of Prah Vihar in April, 1966 and the appearance of evidence that the Thais were actively abetting the Khmer Serai.

Cambodia re-evaluated the Thai threat in the light of the most recent crisis in Southeast Asia, which can be said to have begun with the events of 1960-61 in Laos. Cambodia's concern, and even obsession, with Thailand derives from historic Thai attempts at territorial aggrandizement. But while Thailand appeared rooted in its allegiance to the Western alliance and to SEATO, Cambodia's policy of neutrality seemed to be an effective defensive tool. There was no guarantee, however, that Thailand would maintain a consistent orientation in foreign policy. Thailand had long maintained its independence by a calculated policy of trimming the sails of state to the prevailing political wind. Even after Thailand became a member of SEATO, it gave periodic signs of a shift away from the existing alignments. A neutralist trend was clearly visible during 1958, and this indication of deviation in foreign policy may help explain the Cambodian decision to recognize China in July of that year. On July 14, a coup in Iraq ended the Bagdad Pact, the Middle Eastern equivalent of SEATO. Thai reaction to this event consisted of an outbreak of rumors that a pro-neutralist coup was imminent. To Cambodia, this seemed to portend the departure of Thailand from SEATO. Sihanouk may have then acted on impulse to assure Cambodia's future against a Thailand no longer regarded as a pariah by Peking, considering that it would be advisable to permit a Chinese ambassador in Phnom Penh in return for assurance against Thailand.[21]

No leftist coup materialized in Thailand, but instead Marshal Sarit came to power, probably to forestall just such an eventuality. The position of the Thai Government, even following the Sarit coup, could not be taken for granted. Whenever there was serious doubt as to the degree of backing Thailand could expect from the United States—particularly after United States acceptance of the principles of neutralization for Laos, with Communist participation in its government—there were public murmurings about the need to follow what was euphemistically described as a "traditional policy." One such statement came from the Minister of the Interior, General Praphas, in September, 1962.[22]

Sihanouk has made frequent references to the skill of the Thai "in slipping from one verge, from one bank to the other."[23] He has commented, "We know that our Siamese neighbors are the champions of the world in the business of political tacking and of changing alliances and that they are absolutely unbeatable in the art of making their ship sail in the direction of the prevailing wind." Pointedly, he went on to say, "Today this wind is undeniably that of the East." [24] Sihanouk regarded with grave apprehension the prospect of Thailand becoming sympathetically disposed toward the Chinese People's Republic. He has made no secret of his conviction that Cambodia's political well-being is due "to the fact that a happy chance has placed our country outside the camp in which our neighbors find themselves," and that Thailand's close association with the United States makes it possible for Cambodia to call on the support of the Communist countries—support Sihanouk describes as "so decisive for our survival." [25] He regards the alliance between Thailand (and South Viet-Nam) and the United States as vital to Cambodia's security. If they shifted their Cold War position in response to a change in the Southeast Asian balance of power, they would undermine the conditions for the practice of neutrality. Sihanouk's fears of such a prospect were lent substance during conversations with Mao Tse-tung, who showed himself rather well disposed toward the Thais.[26] Sihanouk has no illusions that a change in Thailand's political orientation "would do away with or even attenuate, however little, their expansionist and Khmerocidal aims." [27]

There might appear to be a certain contradiction between Sihanouk's oft-repeated remark that the United States has encouraged Thailand in pursuing hostile aims against Cambodia and his fear that Thailand might detach itself from political association with the United States. In fact, he is simply recognizing the existence of two threats, one of which has to be endured in order to bring into being countervailing forces to check it. Sihanouk has commented on the paradox of an America which, on the one hand, furnishes Cambodia's adversaries with material means to threaten national existence but which, on the other hand, by its very support of these adversaries, constitutes a guarantee for Cambodia's survival.[28] As long as Thailand is involved with an enemy of

China, threats from Thailand can be neutralized with Chinese support. But if Thailand ceased to be an enemy of China, then the prospect of Chinese support for Cambodia would be reduced. Sihanouk has prepared for this eventuality and has pointed out that "the only way for us to get the better of Thailand will be to hasten to rally the Communist camp before it does." [29] In order to cover all situations, Sihanouk is inclined to favor the continued, though restricted, presence of the United States in Thailand, thus ensuring that Thailand remains an enemy of Communist China, but also giving him some freedom of maneuver in case the Communist threat reappears.

SOUTH VIET-NAM

Cambodia's relationship with South Viet-Nam has been more intensely bitter than that with Thailand. The Cambodians considered the Thais no less predatory than the Vietnamese, but cultural differences between the Cambodians and the Vietnamese, and a Vietnamese tendency to be intolerant of Cambodian customs as they shifted their frontier southward and westward, left a greater residual hostility. Cambodian resentment of the Vietnamese was sustained during the period of the French protectorate, when the Vietnamese were brought into Cambodia as plantation workers and minor civil servants. At the present time, there are approximately 300,000 Vietnamese living in Cambodia and playing a commercial role corresponding to that of the overseas Chinese. The Cambodian Government—aware of their backing for Son Ngoc Thanh, who is part Vietnamese, and resenting the activities of the Viet-Minh—keeps this minority under constant surveillance.

The southern third of Viet-Nam, known as Cochinchina during the French period, was part of the Khmer Kingdom until the late seventeenth century, when it succumbed to Annamite colonization. Even though this territory forms the major portion of South Viet-Nam, the Cambodian Government has never ceased to assert its sovereign rights. When France agreed to the establishment of a unitary state in Viet-Nam in March, 1949, the Cambodian representatives to the Assembly of the French Union objected to the inclusion in it of Cochinchina. They claimed that its attachment to Viet-Nam would mean the end of political and cultural guarantees accorded to the large Khmer minority native to the region. The Cambodian Government raised similar objections again when Cambodia became nominally independent under the provisions of the Franco-Khmer Treaty the following November. Despite the failure of their protests to elicit a response, the Cambodians continued to press objections to the changed status of Cochinchina.[30] During the closing stages of the Geneva Conference, Cambodian Foreign Minister Tep Phan announced that the final declaration, which stipulated respect for the territorial integrity of Viet-Nam, did not "imply the abandonment of such legitimate rights as Cambodia might assert with regard to certain regions of South Viet-Nam about which Cambodia has made express reservations." [31] He went on to assert that the Cambodian-Vietnamese border had been established by unilateral act of France and that Cambodia could only respect Viet-Nam's territorial integrity subject to certain adjustments and regularizations of the border. This statement provoked an emphatic declaration of opposition to the Cambodian position from the Democratic Republic of Viet-Nam which, under the Geneva Agreements, was to succeed to that part of Viet-Nam north of the 17th Parallel.

The Cambodian Government is no doubt aware that it has no prospect of realizing its territorial claim, although it has never relinquished those demands. Indeed, it brought them to the attention of the United Nations in 1958. Cambodia's irredentist claims are also related to nonterritorial issues. A major concern is the large Khmer minority (the Khmer Krom), living in the western provinces of what was formerly Cochinchina. The Cambodian Government has complained incessantly about the harsh treatment accorded the Khmer Krom, charging that "a systematic racial policy is being implemented with the obvious intention of eventually eliminating all traces likely to testify to the Cambodian character of the Cochinchina territory." [32] After the early 1960's—with an increase in Viet-Cong activity in South Viet-Nam, which brought intimidation and terror from both insurgents and government forces—a small but steady stream of refugees across the frontier substantiated Cambodian charges. Speaking before the Sixteenth Session of the United Nations General Assembly in September, 1961, Sihanouk accused the South Vietnamese Government of adopting a deliberate policy of cultural extinction against the Khmer Krom, who numbered, Sihanouk claimed, about 600,000. Successive governments in South Viet-Nam have denied all charges of discrimination and have refused to concede a special status to the Khmer minority. Their position has been that there are no Cambodians living in Viet-Nam, but only Vietnamese of Khmer origin. They insist that these persons enjoy the same rights as other Vietnamese citizens and that they are an integral part of the Vietnamese nation. It is just this concept of integration to which the Cambodian Government objects.

The South Vietnamese have retaliated with allegations that the Vietnamese minority within Cambodia has been the object of discrimination. In May, 1956, the Cambodian Government implemented a law excluding aliens from eighteen occupations; this affected many Vietnamese. The Saigon Government responded by providing the dispossessed with relief and offering to repatriate those who wished to leave Cambodia. In the Cambodian press there have been, on occasion, veiled threats of retaliation against the Vietnamese minority in return for the treatment of the Khmers in South Viet-Nam.[33]

Cambodia and South Viet-Nam have also quarreled over the issue of certain off-shore islands in the Gulf of Siam. Cambodia first raised the matter in a complaint to the International Control Commission, charging Viet-Nam with having attempted to occupy the islands from November, 1955.[34] The dispute has never been settled. The Control Commission could confirm only that the exact location of the boundary between Cambodian and Vietnamese islands in the Gulf of Siam was in dispute and that the local Cambodian authorities were unable to provide conclusive proof of ownership. The original intrusion by Vietnamese could have been intended as retaliation to the Cambodian claims in Cochinchina or could have been unplanned. The Cambodian Government chose to regard the intrusions and subsequent claims to ownership as one more demonstration of Vietnamese expansionism at Cambodian expense. Until 1964, this feeling was substantiated by Sihanouk's failure to elicit a denial from the Government of North Viet-Nam that it regarded the islands as Vietnamese national territory.[35] In 1964, North Viet-Nam finally conceded Cambodia's right to the islands, though not in a formal agreement.

Cambodian anxiety had a specific as well as a general orientation. Before 1960, when the port at Sihanoukville was opened, Cambodia had no outlet to the Gulf of Siam and was virtually totally dependent on the port of Saigon and the Mekong River for its external trade. Sihanoukville, constructed with French assistance, was intended to relieve this dependence. Work began in 1955, the same year in which the dispute over the islands arose. Cambodia regarded the South Vietnamese claims to the off-shore islands—which were in the vicinity of the new port—as an attempt to establish a position commanding the waters leading to Sihanoukville and so threaten Cambodia's efforts to achieve economic independence. Cambodia was alarmed at the prospect of South Viet-Nam's using the islands as a springboard to Sihanoukville. Sihanouk claimed that "the loss of the islands and the territorial waters which surround them would lead to the stifling of the port of Kompong Som (Sihanoukville) and very soon to the end of our independence." [36] The blockade of the Mekong by South Viet-Nam early in 1956 demonstrated Cambodia's economic vulnerability and the necessity to develop the Sihanoukville outlet.

In March, 1960, the Saigon Government called on Cambodia formally to renounce possession of seven of the off-shore islands, including three near Sihanoukville. It did not back up its claim by force, but in Cambodia—where Vietnamese are regarded with pathological dread—these claims, together with sporadic intrusions, are regarded as a sufficient indication of evil intent. The Cambodian Government would like to see the Vietnamese completely removed from the island of Koh Tral (Phu Quoc), formerly part of the colony of Cochinchina. This island is occupied by the South Vietnamese, and the Cambodian Government regards it, perhaps unjustifiably, as sufficiently close to the approaches to Sihanoukville to be used to blockade the port. In April, 1960, the Cambodian delegate to the Conference on the law of the sea in Geneva claimed that Koh Tral (Phu Quoc) was an integral part of Cambodian territory.[37]

Cambodian attempts to avoid economic dependence on Viet-Nam began soon after the reimposition of French authority in 1946. The French were prevailed upon to develop Phnom Penh as a river port (on the Mekong), and the first ships tied up there in April, 1947. At present, Sihanoukville has six berths for ocean-going vessels, but is unable to meet all Cambodia's transport needs. Cambodia would consequently be hit badly by any blockage of the Mekong. In November, 1964, Sihanouk claimed that his government had not recognized North Viet-Nam and the National Liberation Front because he was afraid South Viet-Nam would retaliate by blocking the Mekong.[38]

Border violations have been a recurrent factor in the mutual hostility between Cambodia and South Viet-Nam. During 1956-57, the border violations were caused chiefly by South Vietnamese President Ngo Dinh Diem's attempts to consolidate the position of his regime at the expense of politico-religious sects. Incidents occurred when members of such sects were pursued by South Vietnamese troops to the Cambodian side of the frontier. In June, 1958, following a South Vietnamese penetration several kilometers into Stung Treng Province, Cambodia complained to the International Control Commission. The Commission found that the South Vietnamese soldiers had shifted boundary markers to Cambodia's disadvantage, possibly to cover their tracks.[39] The violation caused a flurry in Phnom Penh, particularly when the ICC ruled that it was not competent to condemn South Viet-Nam. (On this occasion, the ICC was hamstrung because of the position adopted by the Canadian representative.) The Cambodian Government interpreted the Commission's reluctance to act as evidence of a Western conspiracy to undermine Cambodia's territorial integrity. The following month, Cambodia recognized the Chinese People's Republic. The Stung Treng episode probably contributed to that action; indeed, in 1961, Sihanouk went so far as to announce that the establishment of diplomatic relations with Peking was a direct consequence of South Viet-Nam's violation of Cambodian territory in June, 1958.[40]

Border problems still plague Cambodian-Vietnamese relations, despite intermittent attempts to negotiate outstanding issues. A particular difficulty has been the undue sensitivity of Prince Sihanouk to press comment from Saigon. He canceled a visit to South Viet-Nam in 1958 because of an alleged offense by the Viet-Nam News Agency. President Diem's brother, Ngo Dinh Nhu visited Phnom Penh in August, 1958, but his discussions with Sihanouk were inconclusive. Sihanouk did travel to Saigon a year later, but he reached no agreement on border control with South Viet-Nam, and intensification of Viet-Cong activities tended to aggravate the situation. The South Vietnamese were now increasingly suspicious of Cambodia because of its signature, in November, 1958, of a trade and payments agreement with North Viet-Nam. Although Cambodia formally denied that it was contemplating political ties with North Viet-Nam, the agreement was not calculated to provide a foundation for mutual trust between Cambodia and South Viet-Nam.

Relations between the two nations continued to be plagued by two issues. First, there was the South Vietnamese charge that the Viet-Cong was using Cambodian territory as a sanctuary for training and rest camps. No one denied that the Viet-Cong moved both ways across the border, but the South Vietnamese charges related to emplacements and camps. The Cambodian Government went out of its way to demonstrate that it was policing the border to the best of its ability. In September, 1961, an engagement took

place between units of the Cambodian Army and the Viet-Cong
in the province of Svay Rieng, which borders South Viet-Nam. It
was reported that a Viet-Cong base spread over an area of a mile
was destroyed during the fighting.[41] The Cambodian Government
took great pains to refute inferences that could be drawn from this
clash and accordingly invited members of the International Control Commission and a correspondent of *The New York Times* to
search the area in which Saigon claimed Viet-Cong emplacements
were situated. The observers found no evidence of permanent
Viet-Cong bases, and their reports vindicated the Cambodian
position.[42]

The results of the expedition did not satisfy the authorities in
Saigon, who suggested the appointment of mixed border patrols
to police the frontier. Sihanouk refused to consider this proposal,
claiming that joint action against the Communist insurgents would
compromise his country's neutral position. In 1961, the Western-
backed right wing in Laos had collapsed, and the National Liberation Front in South Viet-Nam had become increasingly active.
Sihanouk had no wish to see the conflict in South Viet-Nam spread
to the Cambodian side of the border; he had already expressed
his anxiety at the prospect of internationalization and extension of
the Laotian conflict.[43] Sihanouk was moving steadily toward the
belief that the days of the West were numbered in Southeast Asia,
and he had no desire to offend those who appeared likely to be the
victors in the conflicts affecting the area, in particular the National
Liberation Front.

The second cause of friction arose from the first. South Vietnamese security forces repeatedly violated the Cambodian border
while pursuing the Viet-Cong. These intrusions frequently had
tragic consequences for the civilian population on the Cambodian
side of the border, and the Cambodian Government regarded the
actions as punitive measures directed against itself. The American
"advisers" to the South Vietnamese Army also participated in the
raids, and the diplomatic break between Cambodia and the
United States in May, 1965, was ascribed in part to American par-

ticipation in the bombing of Cambodian villages. In July, 1965, the International Control Commission published a report in which it presented evidence that the armed forces of the Republic of South Viet-Nam were responsible for the border violations. The ICC reported 375 incidents in 1964, and 385 in the first five months of 1965. The Commission unanimously concluded that "none of these incidents were provoked by the Royal Government of Cambodia." [44]

Underlying the antagonism with which the Cambodian Government regards the South Vietnamese is the conviction that its governments have actively engaged in subversion against the Khmer state. The Cambodian Government revealed early in 1959 that the Governor of Siemreap Province, Dap Chhuon Machulpich, had attempted an ill-fated insurrection against the government. His brother survived the abortive coup and implicated Ngo Trong Hieu, the diplomatic representative of South Viet-Nam in Phnom Penh. The *coup manqué* followed soon after the defection of Sam Sary, the former ambassador in London. The following August, a bomb concealed in a parcel addressed to the Queen exploded in an antechamber of the Royal Palace, killing the Chief of Protocol and two members of the palace staff. The events of 1959 lend substance to the recurrent charges by Cambodia against the regimes of Thailand and South Viet-Nam.

Enough has been written to demonstrate the basic antipathy that exists between Cambodia and its neighbors to the east and west. The causes of conflict are rooted in the histories of all three countries, but their present unhappy relationship is also affected by contemporary problems.

LAOS

Cambodia's relations with its third neighbor, Laos, have been generally limited and more friendly than not. Recent Cambodian interest in Laos has been dictated by the success of Pathet Lao forces in consolidating their position in the country. Cambodia's attitude toward Laos is at once benevolent and patronizing, but the prospect of being bordered by a third antagonist that has Communist backing causes certain foreboding. Sihanouk has always regarded Laos as one of the countries in Southeast Asia that it would be most desirable to neutralize. Cambodian involvement and initiative in attempting to effect a solution to the intractable problem of Laos will be discussed below. Meanwhile, of late, the situation in Laos has jelled, and its future relationship to Cambodia will depend on the outcome of events in Viet-Nam.

The Powers and Neutrality

In practice, Cambodia's neutrality was intended to provide for security in the Cold War by permitting it to seek an appropriate counter to an external threat. Cambodia did not anticipate such a threat from a fellow neutral, but from adherents of the two Cold War camps. By rejecting Cold War alignments, it expected to gain sufficient freedom of maneuver to solicit assistance from the Cold War enemy of whatever country threatened it. The practical application of this policy, however, did not involve alternative appeals to one side or the other; revealed threats did not fit into a neat pattern of alternating menace.

The initial threat from the Communist Viet-Minh had been effectively checked by the Geneva Agreements, following which Cambodia had common borders with allies of the West who were also traditional antagonists. This geopolitical restructuring removed the immediate likelihood of external Communist intervention, but still presented a security problem. In order to demonstrate its independence and genuine neutrality, Cambodia entered into relations with Communist countries. As quarrels with Thailand and South Viet-Nam increased in scope and intensity, so these Communist contacts increased in importance as sources of countervailing power. At the same time, its relations with the United States suffered accordingly.

The United States was inevitably drawn into the quarrels be-

tween Cambodia and its neighbors. Both Thailand and South
Viet-Nam were firm adherents of the anti-Communist alliance and
beneficiaries of the economic bounty of the United States. Their
enmity toward Cambodia and their fundamental disapproval of
its foreign policy were evident. As the Cambodian Government
became increasingly convinced of the malpractices and evil intentions of its neighbors, it tended to believe that the United States
was in some way involved in these transgressions. Sihanouk expected his neighbors to behave like obedient puppets of their
American master; but American aid did not, in fact, necessarily
convey political control. A man like Ngo Dinh Diem, for example,
was never a puppet of the American Government.[45] Sihanouk
could understand this difficulty in his own case, but seemed unwilling to show the same sympathy for the United States in its
relations with its allies, Cambodia's neighbors. In public statements, he depicted Thailand and South Viet-Nam as satellites of
the United States, implying that America had the power to unleash
or restrain these so-called puppets almost at will.[46] Cambodia assumed that the difficulties it experienced with Thailand and South
Viet-Nam would continue only as long as the United States wished
them to continue. Sihanouk seemed unable or unwilling to appreciate that the Thais and South Vietnamese were capable of direct-
ing and controlling their own hostile policies toward their neighbor
and that, on occasion, their actions were simply responses to outbursts by Sihanouk which had been construed as provocations.

Sihanouk's difficulties with the United States stem from the very
early days of association. He received no comfort or encouragement from Dulles in 1953, when he sought American support for
Cambodia's national demands. In 1953, as during the rest of the
1950's, the United States tended to treat Sihanouk as a petty
princeling of little significance. One reason for this lack of deference was a series of revelations in the French press seeking to
discredit his diplomatic endeavors by overemphasizing his leisure
activities and his personal eccentricities. He was then a young
man whose manner tended to disguise an acute political sense;

the Americans assessed him at face value. This was certainly the case with the American ambassador accredited to Phnom Penh after the Geneva Conference, Robert McClintock. He behaved toward Sihanouk as might an executive of the United Fruit Company toward the president of a banana republic. Failure to appreciate the sensitive nature of the Cambodian leader left a substantial legacy of insults, which Sihanouk continually disinters and reinterprets in racist terms.[47]

Sihanouk is acutely conscious of the contrast between the glorious period of Khmer history and the international position of contemporary Cambodia. He talks at times of restoring Cambodia's past grandeur and is unduly sensitive to personal slights that reflect on himself and his country. He is tormented by the type of American comment that depicts him as the little "clown-king" of a backward pocket kingdom. He is continually the object of what he considers calumny and distortion by American magazines. An article in *Newsweek* in April, 1965, justified, in part, the severing of diplomatic relations with the United States Government.

In spite of instances of coarse treatment by American diplomats, offensive press coverage, and unfortunate personal experiences while visiting the United States,[48] it would be an exaggeration to attribute the progressive deterioration of Cambodian-American relations solely to Sihanouk's hurt dignity. He is a skillful politician, and it is believed that his increasing bellicosity toward the United States reflected a re-evaluation of the power balance in Southeast Asia. When he became convinced that the drift of events could not be controlled by the United States, he permitted his personal emotions to control his public utterances. This became very apparent after the Laotian settlement in July, 1962, when Sihanouk sought without success to secure an international guarantee for his country's neutrality and territorial integrity. A negative response from the United States—in contrast to the friendly reaction of China—left him angry. Sihanouk's outbursts were prompted by a belief that the United States, in pursuing what he considered a policy of blind anti-Communism, had spoiled a chance to neutralize Laos. It had provoked international intervention in a conflict that could spill over Cambodia's frontiers, and, by sponsoring an unpopular dictatorship, as in South Viet-Nam, it was abetting a revolutionary process that could also cross the Cambodian border. Indeed, the continuation of this process would bring Cambodia face to face with a reunited Communist Viet-Nam—a fearful prospect. Sihanouk's posture toward the United States thus reflected annoyance at past insults and misdeeds, plus exasperation at a policy whose effects appeared to jeopardize Cambodia.

Cambodia's relationship with the Chinese People's Republic had a much more harmonious aspect. The Chinese were skillful in their handling of Sihanouk and took considerable care to accord him proper deference and respect. He was never subjected to the humiliating encounters that he had experienced in the United States. China, of course, was not handicapped by being allied to countries that seemed to pose direct threats to Cambodia, and it was happy to exploit a situation in which it could embarrass the United States by joining with Cambodia in denouncing the aggressive intent of Thailand and South Viet-Nam.

The initiative in encouraging the association owed much to Chou En-lai's efforts at Bandung. Before it ever became necessary to solicit expressions of Chinese support, the Chinese Premier had indicated his willingness to look with tolerance on a nonaligned Cambodia. Cambodia had no desire to invite the antagonism of Peking and was amenable to playing the role desired.[49] It has been pointed out that "A hostile attitude toward Communist China was a luxury their statesmen would have felt unable to afford even had they wished it." [50] China demanded of Cambodia only one condition in return for its benevolent outlook, and that was to exclude an American military presence. This was a small price to pay for a measure of security against the Vietnamese and local Communists.[51]

During what can be described as the first step in the practice of neutrality, Chinese assistance was not needed to restrain the Hanoi regime. It was not until after 1960 that the relationship with China was more closely connected with ensuring territorial integrity in the event of a reunited Viet-Nam. Throughout the Sino-Cambodian association, China has been able to play the role of the benevolent protector. There were tangible benefits from this relationship. Cambodia received economic assistance, although this did not compare with the bounty of the United States. Economic aid and visits by Chinese luminaries helped to stablize the internal situation. Sihanouk was able to neutralize his domestic left wing by demonstrating that his neutrality was of an independent and anticolonial variety. Contacts with Chinese did have some initial disturbing effects on Cambodia's Chinese community (estimated at 300,000), but in general, the Chinese Government behaved as a model of rectitude. It provided no comfort for left-wing dissidents, and it did not offer sanctuary in Peking for Communist exiles. As the association developed, China took steps to encourage Cambodia's Chinese minority to be model citizens and not to engage in political activities.[52]

From the political enthronement of Sihanouk in September, 1955, until the deterioration of security conditions in Southeast Asia after 1960, the practice of neutrality corresponded to theory. The one-sided appeal was a consequence of the apparent one-sided threat, and this meant that relations with the United States suffered accordingly. The Communist threat had receded, and the political balance seemed to favor the West. The principal source of conflict was with Cambodia's anti-Communist neighbors, and this circumstance tended to dictate the orientation of the Cambodian response. It was still desirable, however, to maintain a balance of international associations. If there was no American military presence within Cambodia, aid teams and a military assistance group were indications that Cambodia was not committed in one direction.

With the evident failure of the United States to have its way in Laos after 1960, and the growth of insurgency in South Viet-Nam, the practice of neutrality began to take on a different aspect. National priorities remained the same, but it became increasingly apparent that Cambodia's prospects of providing for security lay in establishing an accommodation with the country that could exercise a dominating influence in Southeast Asia. There was decreasing confidence in the United States' ability to play such a role and increasing recognition that the future lay with China.

5

The Style of Neutrality

Cambodian foreign policy has been explained so far in terms of internal imperatives and external geopolitical factors. But Cambodia's neutrality also reflects the individualism of the country's principal luminary. As a doctrine of foreign policy, neutrality safeguards national interests and, at the same time, satisfies Sihanouk's personal aspirations.

The Legacy of Kingship

Prince Norodom Sihanouk came to the throne of Cambodia in April, 1941; he was then eighteen. He was not the heir apparent to the late King, Monivong Sisowath, but was chosen according to a French-instituted method of royal selection that enabled the colonial governors to bypass the direct line for reasons of political expediency. The Norodom branch of the family had been bypassed when the father of Monivong Sisowath was enthroned. In 1941, the Norodom branch was reinstated because it suited French political purposes. The French authorities considered Prince Monireth—the son of the late King, and Sihanouk's uncle —too politically conscious. They chose Sihanouk, ostensibly to restore the senior branch of the royal family, but in fact because they expected him to be a pliable instrument of the colonial administration.

To be king in Cambodia, even under French colonial rule, is no ordinary royal experience. The Cambodian throne is associated with the divine kingship of Hindu cosmological tradition. The French, for reasons of their own, sustained the sacred trappings of the monarchy and even helped to elevate its status. They enhanced the majesty of the throne and skillfully disguised the extent to which the royal incumbent was a servant of the colonial regime. The king accordingly lived in a rarefied atmosphere of utmost deference and was regarded with religious reverence by his subjects. Norodom Sihanouk experienced this kind of attention at an impressionable age, and it is not surprising that he came to accept flattery and praise as part of his everyday life. But when Sihanouk chose to step into the domestic political arena after his success in the Royal Crusade for Independence, his position was no longer a reflection of the artificial life of the royal court: He enjoyed genuine popular support because he had effectively associated his divine being with the fortunes of his nation. He thus reinvigorated a traditional role that was none the less deep-rooted because of his modern outlook. The recurrent cabinet crises after 1955 were a product of the political immaturity of Cambodian politicians, but their effect was to demonstrate time and time again Sihanouk's indispensable position as leader of the nation.

When Sihanouk abdicated his throne, he did not lose his divine attributes. He was the King among politicians. Revered as the father of independence and as the savior of his people, he had performed those functions expected of a Cambodian monarch. His authority, which was based on popular affection, reflected traditional values and exceptional personal qualities. He was genuinely in touch with his people. Indeed, he has made it a regular practice to visit again and again the most outlying provinces and to show himself to the peasantry. Imagine the impression on sedentary villagers made by Sihanouk descending from the skies by helicopter as if on the wings of the mythological Garuda eagle.

When he goes among the people in this way, distributing bolts of cloth or taking part in ancient rituals, he represents the god-King of Angkor vintage, whose sacred presence if imbibed will bestow good fortune. In Cambodia, Sihanouk is omnipotent.

After the elections of September, 1955, the principal opposition ceased to exist as a going political concern, and by the time of the next elections, in 1958, it was nonexistent. The only organized opposition to Sangkum was the left-wing and allegedly pro-Communist Pracheachon Party. It did not, however, contest the 1962 or the 1966 elections, and on each occasion Sangkum took all seats in the Assembly. There is, therefore, no effective opposition to Sangkum, and within Sangkum Sihanouk's position is generally beyond challenge. A measure of opposition and dissension does exist within Sangkum, and Sihanouk has had to accommodate the growing number of educated younger members who feel that the path to preferment is encumbered with too many relics of the *ancien régime*. Sihanouk's appeal to the younger elite is genuine, but he has to work harder to obtain the desired response from this group, which is less rooted in tradition than the vast majority of the population. These young people tend to be more anti-imperialist and oriented to the left than Sihanouk. They lack his flexible approach to foreign policy, and their more rigid commitment to an ideological line could be an obstacle to speedy maneuver in the national interest. For the time being, however, the young as well as the old faithfully support Sihanouk and his foreign policy initiatives.

It is necessary to appreciate Sihanouk's internal position to understand his international outlook: One is clearly a reflection, at least in part, of the other. Within Cambodia, Sihanouk has come to expect popular adoration as an everyday occurrence; such reverence is part of his psychological sustenance. When he turns his attention to international politics, he finds it difficult to shrug off this conditioning. One can say without exaggeration that he is congenitally incapable of acting as a member of an alliance or the subordinate of a larger grouping. He is certainly not content to be the leader of just one more country in the neutral bloc. He has pointed out that Cambodia has no inclination to "belong to the 'club' of the large neutralists, because it would have no role to play in such a club." Within such an association, he envisages Cambodia's occupying a position similar to that of Greece or the Benelux countries within NATO.[1] Sihanouk, who is only too conscious of the size and population of Cambodia, is not content to see his country as another neutral also-ran. He has no wish to see Cambodia submerged beneath the increasing weight of newly independent states, many of whom are wealthier and more populous than Cambodia. Thus, while Sihanouk will attend international gatherings of neutrals and Afro-Asians, he takes care to maintain an individual pose.

Sihanouk's search for distinction reflects the contrast between his domestic personal standing and Cambodia's international position, and at times he tends to act as if the world outside ought to correspond to the Cambodian internal condition. He has been encouraged in this direction by the Chinese and French governments, which have been extremely skillful in exploiting his personal sensibilities. The French, who at one time reviled Sihanouk, now treat him with the utmost respect, particularly as de Gaulle and Sihanouk agree about the type of settlement necessary to stabilize the Indochinese area. From the beginning of their association, the Chinese have gone out of their way to pander to Sihanouk. The flattering attention of this great Asian power makes the world outside parallel the Cambodian scene. Sihanouk, leader of a country of less than six million people, was invited in October, 1965, to be the guest of honor at celebrations honoring the sixteenth anniversary of the Chinese People's Republic. To a national leader unaccustomed to the adulation that is part of the Cambodian political process, this occasion would have been a moving experience. To Sihanouk, it was a mark of external recognition that corresponded to his domestically conditioned view of personal grandeur.[2]

Unfortunately, Sihanouk does not always receive such deference, and it is not only the West that is guilty of what he regards as acts of *lèse-majesté*. In October, 1965, the Soviet Government was too busy to receive Sihanouk, who had expected to attend the celebrations marking the anniversary of the Bolshevik Revolution on November 7. Sihanouk had made some rather injudicious remarks in Peking about the Soviet Union's policy toward Viet-Nam,[3] but he nevertheless regarded the humiliation as "a virtual provocation for a rupture in relations." [4] Sihanouk had been used to affronts only from the West, and he commented bitterly that never—even at the height of their dispute—had the United States allowed itself "to humiliate me in this manner." [5]

Sihanouk seems to be incapable of tolerating any act that disturbs his self-esteem. He reacted to the Soviet snub as if his personal pride had been deeply wounded. Such wounds have been a more common experience at the hands of Western governments, with the exception of France in recent years. The United States and Britain seem either unwilling or unable to play the role desired by Sihanouk, whom they are disposed to regard as unstable and unreliable. Difficulties with the West are not simply the results of policy disagreements or even attacks on British and American embassies and information centers. The Western experience has been that one cannot expect normal diplomatic behavior in dealings with Sihanouk. It is necessary to relate diplomatic performance to Sihanouk's personal style in the role of a twentieth-century god-king. Sihanouk has a tendency to conduct diplomatic exchanges in the style of a Byzantine potentate rather than according to the rules established by the Congress of Vienna. He is capable of treating ambassadors like lowly messenger boys and has been known to subject them out of their hearing to periodic torrents of verbal abuse—disturbing behavior to those accustomed to the procedure of the Court of St. James's. British and American diplomats, especially, consider Phnom Penh a graveyard for reputations. Before the diplomatic break with the United States in May, 1965, an American ambassador accredited to Phnom Penh was met at Pochentong Airport by a junior protocol officer. He was then kept waiting for three weeks, while a date was set for him to present his credentials. At the very last moment, Sihanouk refused to receive the ambassador, in order to demonstrate his displeasure toward the United States Government. Sihanouk seems to have little conception of the function of an ambassador. He does not seem to appreciate an ambassador's potential for conciliation, which he could exploit to Cambodia's advantage. He does not seem able to respect confidential approaches; an ambassador who tries to communicate with him takes the risk that his *démarche* will become public property within a few hours, possibly even broadcast to the world over Phnom Penh Radio. Sihanouk has small regard for secret diplomacy, preferring a more open, and even spectacular, style of political communication.

While he likes to parade his hates and to utter invective from the public platform, in private Sihanouk tends to compensate for his virulence. He occasionally entertains an ambassador he has just subjected to a vicious personal attack in the Khmer language as if nothing untoward had happened. The diplomat so treated is rarely sure of his position, which is probably Sihanouk's intention.

Sihanouk's experience during the Royal Crusade for Independence may account for his attitude toward political communication. It is quite possible that he prefers journalists to diplomats because he found during the Crusade that public diplomacy was more effective than the secret variety. His treatment by American and some European journalists, however, has disturbed his self-esteem. The contrast between the incessant adulation in the columns of the Cambodian press and the periodic sarcasm at his expense in Western newspapers is frequently too much for him to endure. His pet abominations are the American magazines *Time* and *Newsweek*, which he feels are engaged in a constant campaign of vilification. Sihanouk has firm control of the Cambodian communication media, so he may find it difficult to appreciate that the American press is not guided by the American Government. He has confessed, "Until I breathe my last, never will any of those injustices, scorn, belittlements, shameful slanders be erased from my memory." [6] Sihanouk is always ready to react electrically to what he regards as the crude scribblings of ill-informed journalists.

When *The New York Times* commented that the "Cambodian Chief of State has acted with characteristic excitability and imperiousness in initiating a break in relations between Thailand and Cambodia," [7] Sihanouk immediately wrote a stinging reply. He pays scrupulous attention to foreign writings about his country and is quite unwilling to tolerate adverse comment, frequently resorting to a course of action that might be regarded as unbecoming to a chief of state. Besides replying publicly to critical articles in newspapers and magazines, he has personally communicated his reproaches to journalists, often couching his reply more in sorrow than in anger.

Despite his painful dealings with the international press, Sihanouk needs its constant attention. Even adverse comment is publicity, and he seems to thrive on it. Indeed, he is likely to accord better facilities to visiting journalists than to members of the diplomatic corps. Although time and time again he literally screams at the calumnies of the Western press and then excludes their correspondents from Cambodia, it is rarely long before he relents and provides visas allowing some of them to return. Bernard Gordon has suggested, with some justice, that Sihanouk's constant urge to occupy the center of attention and never be taken for granted is intrinsically related to Cambodia's security needs.[8] But such an analysis neglects the fact that Sihanouk is so obsessed with personal and national position that he has found it necessary to enumerate in public all those countries that are either smaller in area than Cambodia or have smaller populations.[9] This obsession with Cambodia's size and population may derive from Sihanouk's awareness of the contrast between the modern Khmer State and the historic empire. He probably pines for the grandeur of past centuries and compensates in the only way possible, by playing to the international gallery.

Deference and Diplomacy

In trying to assess the extent to which Prince Sihanouk is obsessed with symbols of rank and recognition, there is no more

revealing source than his own report on his 1960 visit to the
United States to participate in the unusual and historic Fifteenth
General Assembly of the United Nations, which was distinguished
by the presence of many heads of government and the unconventional behavior of Soviet Premier Nikita Khrushchev. Sihanouk
recounts that his personal participation was unavoidable because
of the number of the national leaders who were attending. He
was clearly piqued, as he has related, that the initiative for this
innovation in representation was attributed to Khrushchev rather
than to himself. "In all modesty, we must recall that Cambodia,
two years before the USSR, in 1958 had already taken this initiative when Norodom Sihanouk sat at the head of the Khmer delegation to the United Nations and was the sole national leader and
head of government present." [10] He makes very plain his resentment of the relatively diminutive status of Cambodia on this occasion, and sneers at the fact that only the gestures of the great
powers were noticed. He continues his bitter monologue by contrasting the punctuality of the Cambodian delegation and the
deliberate dallying of other delegations. He seemed even more
irritated by the large attendance for his speech, which he felt was
due to the fact that the speaker following him was to be British
Prime Minister Harold Macmillan.

Sihanouk had much to say on the speeches that were made
during the session. He condemned most out of hand as being inspired by prejudice or hate, and here his strictures applied equally
to both sides in the Cold War. Indeed, he was somewhat annoyed
with the Communist delegations, because they seemed to reserve
their applause only for the big neutrals. He also expressed himself
disgusted by Khrushchev's behavior, and even more so by the
constant attention showered on the Soviet leader by the American
press. His judgment of his own contribution was more self-right-
eous than modest: "We were the only country to tackle each question, each problem, with objectivity, frankness, and a certain cour-
age in the face of the three great groups." [11]

His comments on the United States were full of spleen, particularly because he felt insufficient provision had been made to accord

him the external symbols appropriate to his self-esteem. He was incensed that he was received at the airport in New York by an under-chief of protocol. He became even more angry when he discovered that Prince Moulay Hassan of Morocco, who was not even a head of state, was received by a more senior official. Insult was added to injury when the police forced Prince Sihanouk's unescorted car to the side of the road to make way for that of Prince Hassan, who was preceded by a siren escort. Sihanouk seemed to have countless experiences of being forced to pull to the side of the road, while more eminent personages, particularly Khrushchev and his satellite entourage, passed by freely. An even more humiliating experience took place when, on departing from the United Nations building, Sihanouk was pushed out of the way by a policeman to allow the more easily recognized Khrushchev to depart. Resentment at such unfortunate treatment was to be expected not merely from Sihanouk but from any other head of state. It is doubtful, however, that any other head of state would have gone so far as to make his feelings publicly known in the same way. Sihanouk appeared to be obsessed with status symbols and the lack of suitably deferential treatment. Whether he was discussing the failure to provide him with motorcycle escorts or the contrast between the solitary police guard at the door to his hotel suite compared with the abundance of uniformed attendants for Indonesian President Sukarno, Sihanouk was constantly attentive to the slightest act of *lèse-majesté* and left no doubt of his burning resentment at such treatment. He also found distasteful the high place accorded to the delegations from newly independent African states. He blamed those states in part for the circus atmosphere of the Fifteenth Assembly, as they were only too ready to follow the clowning example of Khrushchev. His irritation at their position was evident when he exclaimed that in 1953–54 Cambodia was incontestably more independent of France than certain African countries were in 1960, but that Cambodia was not welcomed into the United Nations with the same enthusiasm as the new African states.[12]

Sihanouk's attitude to the countries of the neutralist grouping reveals a similar concern with position and status. He was reluctant to become involved in the neutralist bloc for fear of being submerged beneath the weight of more powerful neutrals. He sought to achieve a position that would differentiate him and his country from the neutrals. Sihanouk sought to explain Cambodia's desire to stay out of any bloc, even a neutral one, in terms of its compromising effect on his country's truly neutral status. He has argued that membership in a bloc is hardly an appropriate position from which to condemn the system of blocs. In terms of profitability, he has claimed that there is nothing to gain by being aligned with the weakest bloc, which is suspect in the eyes of the West and accorded consideration by Communist countries only in so far as it serves their struggle with the capitalist world. Even more realistic is the argument that Cambodia would have no role to play in the neutralist club and that membership in it would involve a loss of liberty of action. He has also been frank enough to admit another reason for not adhering to a so-called neutralist association: The invitation, which came from President Tito of Yugoslavia, to participate in the deliberations of the major neutrals came too late to satisfy his pride. In 1956, he was invited to visit Yugoslavia, and arrived at Brioni while Tito, Nehru, and Nasser—the neutralist triumvirate—were in conference. He was kept waiting until their discussions had ended and then installed in a hotel until he could occupy the quarters Nasser had just vacated. He claims, "I was treated royally but never was there any possibility of one day joining the club of great neutralists." [13] He relates that Yugoslavia sought to promote a meeting of neutrals in 1957, but Cambodia was not on the list of neutral possibles. In 1959, he received invitations to visit the United Arab Republic and Yugoslavia but not to join the neutralist club. Sihanouk has a long memory for alleged slights, and there is little doubt that he regarded the recognition of his neutral eminence as too long delayed. In refusing Tito, he was therefore only paying back in kind the insults accorded him by sins of omission.

Sihanouk has been involved in neutralist causes. For example,

Cambodia has supported China's entry to the United Nations, upheld Indonesia's claims prior to the settlement of the West Irian dispute, and recognized the provisional Algerian Government before the French conceded its independence. However, Cambodia has never been a blind follower of the neutralist camp. Its delegation did not vote for the expulsion and censure of South Africa from the United Nations in 1961. Cambodia enjoys full diplomatic relations with the State of Israel. Of late, out of deference to Communist China, Cambodia's position on some issues—the partial nuclear test-ban treaty, for example—has differed from that of most other neutrals. Its stand, however, was not solely a product of a growing association with Peking. For Cambodia, experience of neutral contacts has mainly taken the form of requests for support on issues that do not always relate to its national needs. There has been little mutuality in the relationship and even a measure of condescension displayed by some neutrals. Sihanouk has remarked, "The Nabobs of the Third World of non-aligned nations have their own problems and have little time to worry about Cambodia." [14] Cambodia has not received support from its neutral associates in its difficulties with Thailand and South Viet-Nam. More recently, Sihanouk pointed out: "It has been noticeable, that when the time comes to substantiate declarations of solidarity by acts, many countries, which go to make up our Third World—and not necessarily the least influential—tend to adopt an extremely reserved (egotistical might be an apter word) attitude in regard to specific problems put to them by brother countries in difficulties." [15]

Like other neutrals, Sihanouk is never so happy as when he is able to play the mediator. He has offered his services on several occasions, and, to his credit, he has achieved a measure of success. His principal accomplishment was in helping to convene the International Conference on Laos, which began in Geneva in May, 1961. He performed more signal service in arranging a meeting between the leaders of the three warring factions in that country. On his return to Cambodia after the opening sessions of the conference, he proclaimed:

Our nation is rightly proud of this role and of a prestige of which we have not tasted since the 14th century and this in defence and justice for a brother country. With this prestige and role, we have certainly surpassed ourselves. For the first time in our history we were called upon to assume responsibilities and accomplish a job of world importance and on an equal footing with the greatest and the smallest.[16]

Sihanouk was invited to attend the meeting in Colombo in December, 1962, which sought to mediate the Sino-Indian border dispute. This conference, however, embarrassed Sihanouk, because of his desire not to become involved in any action the Chinese Government would regard as offensive. Sihanouk has offered to mediate between China and the United States, but neither side has acted on his offer. In 1964, he arranged a meeting in Phnom Penh between Malaysian Prime Minister Tunku Abdul Rahman and Philippine President Macapagal to discuss the Philippine claim to North Borneo. In his search for distinction as an international peacemaker, Sihanouk is no different from the other Third World mediators, but he is more frank than most in revealing his concern with correct treatment and deference.

Sihanouk resents the fact that Phnom Penh has never been the scene of a recognized international gathering. He was very annoyed when it was not chosen as the site for the 1961–62 International Conference on Laos. Since then, Sihanouk has devoted considerable attention to providing Phnom Penh with the facilities necessary for such a conference. He succeeded in arranging for the Indochinese People's Conference to be held in Phnom Penh in March, 1965, but that meeting did not bring Cambodia the kind of fame that one associates with Bandung.

Sihanouk is very sensitive to the failure of neutral leaders to treat Cambodia with the proper respect. He was annoyed by Indonesian President Sukarno's last-minute decision not to attend the Cambodian independence anniversary celebrations in November, 1964. Similarly, he was put out by the inability of figures like President Modibo Keita of Mali and Sékou Touré of Guinea to find time to visit while passing through Southeast Asia. In April, 1965, during the celebrations in Djakarta commemorating the tenth anniversary of the Bandung Conference, Sihanouk found it necessary to lodge a complaint with the Indonesian Government. Sihanouk, who attended these celebrations, was upset to discover that there was an error at Cambodia's expense on a map illustrating the cover of a program: Cambodia appeared as a minute spot, as though its territory had been swallowed up by Thailand and South Viet-Nam. Equally irritating was the failure of the celebration authorities to fly the Cambodian flag at the Djakarta airport alongside those of the countries of the other delegations and at the long time it took to repair this omission. The Indonesian Foreign Minister apologized for what he described as "regrettable errors," but Sihanouk does not easily forget incidents of this nature.

Sihanouk is above all a patriot, but the style of diplomacy through which he seeks to advance his country's interests reflects personal as well as national ambition.

6

Deviation from Nonalignment?

Sihanouk explains Cambodia's foreign policy in terms of geopolitical circumstances. He envisaged neutrality as a policy that would permit flexible response to any dramatic change in circumstances. It was founded on the unproven premise that recourse to the assistance of either the West or the East would be feasible in the event of aggression by a member or members of the opposing bloc. As Sihanouk pointed out, "If, in spite of our manifest good intentions and utter propriety in respect to the blocs, one of these should attack us, then I would be the first to advocate reconsidering our policy and invoking aid from the opponents of our aggressors." [1] It was this untested potential for recourse to alternative sources of assistance, together with the expectation that such assistance would be readily forthcoming, that served as a basic assumption for the practice of neutrality. Above all, Sihanouk's unequivocal declaration of intent was meant to deter those who might consider challenging Cambodia. His aim was to avoid, if possible, having to invoke any such deterrent but rather "to try to maintain an equal balance between the blocs." [2] Indeed, by resorting to the assistance of one of the blocs, Cambodia would have terminated its nonalignment.

According to Sihanouk's theory of neutrality, Cambodia would be able to sustain its desired international position if both sides in the Cold War came to respect its independence, either in their own interests or through the fear of provoking each other. To achieve the ideal balance between the blocs, a balance of power between East and West in the Indochina area was necessary. When Sihanouk enunciated his policy of neutrality, that condition existed. When, however, that balance of power began to tip in one direction, neutrality showed itself capable of almost protean transformation.

Cambodia had become neutral under the favorable circumstances dictated by the Geneva Agreements of 1954. It was not subjected to territorial surgery, as was Viet-Nam, nor was it forced to concede a substantial foothold to pro-Communists, as was Laos. Cambodia did not share a frontier with a Communist state, and Western-supported South Viet-Nam provided a buffer against any physical intervention by the Viet-Minh, who had set up their own puppet regime for Cambodia by 1952. As long as that territorial equilibrium existed, Cambodia could remain neutral. Once it became apparent—as a result of events first in Laos and then in Viet-Nam which the United States seemed incapable of checking—that a new balance would arise, then Cambodia adjusted its concept of neutrality. In his *Foreign Affairs* article, Sihanouk had referred to Cambodia's being "only thinly screened by Laos." [3] It now appeared to him that the screen in question was being removed.

Crisis in Laos

Laos, governed by Prince Souvanna Phouma, had sought to follow a neutral policy after the Geneva Agreements. Peking approved such a policy, especially after November, 1957, when it appeared that the government of Laos would allow the Pathet Lao to participate in national politics. In the supplementary elections of May, 1958, however, leftist candidates won a majority of seats. The subsequent suspension of United States aid caused the fall of Souvanna Phouma and his replacement by a right-wing government determined to force the integration of the Pathet Lao on its own terms. The new government, headed by Phoui Sananikone and backed by the United States, indicated that it would establish military control over those provinces that served as the regroupment areas of the Pathet Lao. That threat involved Laos in the Viet-Nam dispute.

By 1958, insurgency had begun in South Viet-Nam,[4] and southern-born Vietnamese who had gone north after the Geneva settlement were trained and sent back to South Viet-Nam to support the insurgents. The route these men used—now immortalized as the Ho Chi Minh Trail—was through the mountains of eastern Laos. Determined to exclude the Royal Lao Army from this area vital to the effective conduct of insurgency in South Viet-Nam, the North Vietnamese Government after December, 1958, took measures to establish effective control of those parts of the Laotian border through which it was possible to pass to South Viet-Nam, and it moved two companies of regular troops across the border a distance of six miles.[5] The authority of the Laotian Government was more decisively undermined the following May by the defection of a Pathet Lao battalion that had refused to accept the government's terms for integration into the Royal Army. Thereafter, Laos was subject to intermittent armed conflict with the Pathet Lao. Fortified by North Vietnamese assistance, the Pathet Lao consolidated its hold over the northeastern provinces. In the capital, the right-wing forces were ruthlessly determined not to permit any reconciliation with the Pathet Lao. Following the coup by Captain Kong Lê in August, 1960, the Pathet Lao began to extend its military operations in an attempt to increase its bargaining power before any impending negotiations. By early September, its activities reached south of Pakse, where it blew up bridges on the road linking Laos to Cambodia.

The trend of events in Laos after the fall of Souvanna Phouma in 1958 was a cause of great anxiety to Prince Sihanouk. He was alarmed by the prospect of factional conflict degenerating into a civil war that would be sustained by outside interference. From

1959 onward, Sihanouk had made public his concern about a revival of the type of situation that had preceded the Geneva settlement. The danger for Cambodia in this situation was that great power intervention could push the conflict within Laos over its southern border into Cambodia.

Sihanouk was unhappy at the prospect of United States involvement in Laos. His experience with the CIA suggested that if Laos became a so-called right-wing bastion, this might encourage attempts to repeat the exercise with Cambodia. He had little confidence in the ability of the United States to control the situation in Laos. He believed that the United States had spoiled any prospect of a sane balance in Laos, and that, as a consequence, the Communists would press their advantage to Cambodia's northern border. In particular, he believed that the nature of American involvement was not only ineffective but also likely to be provocative. Sihanouk demonstrated his concern in September, 1960, when he brought the question of Laos to the attention of the United Nations General Assembly.[6] He then made an impassioned but unproductive plea for the neutralization of both Laos and Cambodia within a buffer zone that would be guaranteed by the powers concerned. He envisaged some form of insulation, externally provided and based on the willingness of the powers to avoid a head-on collision. Sihanouk pointed out, "Laos does not deserve to be sacrificed with cynicism and brutality on the altar of a diseased anti-Communism, by certain foreign leaders and agents who favor a secession and coldly envisage the abandonment of the north to communism and the creation of an illusionary anti-communist bastion in the south."[7]

The subsequent course of events demonstrated to Sihanouk's satisfaction that American involvement in the Laotian crisis was both provocative and ineffectual. The right-wing forces led by General Phoumi Nosovan and Prince Boun Oum sought to arrogate to themselves the rightful constitutional position and, with American encouragement, launched a countercoup which by December had given them possession of a much battered Vientiane, but the fundamental situation in Laos remained unaltered. Kong Lê had now allied his forces with those of the Pathet Lao and was obtaining Soviet supplies airlifted from Hanoi. In December, the National Liberation Front (NLF) for South Viet-Nam had been formed and Laos—through which insurgent forces infiltrated South Viet-Nam—came to play an increasingly important role in North Viet-Nam's attempts at reunification.

In November and December, 1960, Sihanouk paid official visits to the Soviet Union and China. The joint communiqués issued after each visit indicated that Laos had been a subject of discussion. Sihanouk appeared to obtain greater sympathy for his neutral point of view in Moscow, where he received backing for his recognition of neutral Souvanna Phouma as head of the legitimate government of Laos as well as recognition of the necessity to stand by the Geneva Agreements.[8] By contrast, the section dealing with Laos in the joint communiqué with the Chinese was terse and much less conciliatory in tone. No mention was made of Souvanna Phouma or the Geneva Agreements.[9] The Soviet Union took by far the more active diplomatic role in the Laotian crisis, perhaps because it hoped thereby to retain the allegiance of North Viet-Nam in the developing Sino-Soviet quarrel.[10]

On December 22, the Soviet Government suggested that the Geneva Conference be recalled in order to settle the Laotian question[11] and made it clear that it supported Souvanna Phouma as head of the legal government. On January 1, 1961, Sihanouk took up this proposal in a letter to British Prime Minister Harold Macmillan and other heads of government. He made no secret of his concern that the civil war in Laos was likely to be transformed into an international conflict and envelop Cambodia or that his reasons for wanting to restore peace to Laos were closely related to Cambodia's own security needs. Sihanouk's proposal marked an advance on that of the Soviet Government in that it suggested a meeting of the participants of the Geneva Agreements of 1954 and the nations that made up the International Control Commission as well as any other country that shared a common frontier with Laos.[12] It is interesting to note Sihanouk was also angling for consent to hold the proposed fourteen-nation conference in Phnom Penh.[13]

Sihanouk did not get a positive response from Macmillan, who merely suggested that Sihanouk's proposal for a neutral zone in Laos and Cambodia might receive the attention of any conference convened to deal with Laos. Macmillan felt that the first priority was to put a stop to the fighting and that the only way to bring this about that appeared to have the support of all parties was Nehru's proposal for the immediate re-establishment of the International Control Commission for Laos. If Sihanouk was disappointed by this response, he must have been equally perturbed by the outcome of the ground conflict in Laos during January, 1961, when the Royal Lao troops were pushed off the Plain of Jarres. This defeat indicated the end of any balance of forces within Laos and an inevitable victory for pro-Communist forces. Indeed, the outgoing administration of President Eisenhower had come to admit the possibility of an independent Laos with Pathet Lao participation in the government. In March, the new administration of John F. Kennedy recognized that it had no alternative but to support a neutral and independent Laos and a conference to discuss such an aim. By this time, however, Sihanouk saw little future in discussing a neutrality whose pro-Communist orientation had already been determined on the field of battle.[14] When it was at last agreed to convene a conference on Laos in Geneva, he had given up all hope of a genuinely neutral neighbor.[15]

The Soviet Union, China, and North Viet-Nam had almost immediately supported Sihanouk's proposal. The British held out until March 23, by which time the United States had recognized that a conference was preferable to total capitulation by the forces it was backing.[16] The Soviet Union proposed that the conference should take place in Phnom Penh, but Geneva was chosen, despite Cambodian enthusiasm for the proposal.[17] When the conference was eventually convened in May, 1961, Sihanouk was compensated with the privilege of making the opening address.

Sihanouk used the occasion to reiterate his desire that any neutralization of Laos should be extended to Cambodia, preferably in the form of his proposed neutral zone.[18] He failed, however, to command the attention he thought his contribution to the enterprise merited. His proposals for neutralization on Austrian lines did not gain the approval of the Communist states and neutrals such as India and Burma had little time for his ideas, which, according to one author, "expressed Cambodia's interests and anxieties more accurately than the requirements of non-alignment." [19] Toward the end of June, he did arrange a meeting of the three Laotian factions in Zurich, but his praiseworthy efforts to bring about a reconciliation between the contending Laotians went almost unnoticed at Geneva.

Sihanouk returned to Phnom Penh on July 8 and immediately reiterated his anxiety about the state of affairs in Laos. He said, "The gravest and most unsettling feature in this Laotian affair was the threat of a general war which would soon emerge from the Laotian cadre to spread and ravage countries near Laos and even distant areas. In such an eventuality, our country would have been and still could be one of the very first victims of the internationalization of the Laotian conflict." [20] Sihanouk had been mortally offended by the complete lack of response to his initiatives in Geneva and by the fact that they had been considered "neither reasonable nor useful but premature." Sihanouk could find nothing good to say about any of the other countries attending the conference and made sure that his own account of his *deus ex machina* activities would be recorded for Cambodian posterity. He claimed the main credit for progress at the conference, asserting that his arrival in Geneva had put the conference back on the rails. The Cambodian Government then published a series of documents setting out its proposals for a Laotian settlement but which, it claimed, "Prince Norodom Sihanouk refrained from presenting following opposition from the Laotians and great powers." [21]

A Political Reappraisal

Sihanouk returned to Cambodia full of foreboding for his kingdom. One of his first actions was to intensify pressure against local Communists to ensure that internal security was bolstered against contagion from Laos. Sihanouk argued that pro-Communist activities within Cambodia were conducted through the Pracheachon Party, formed in 1955 by ex-Issarraks and Viet-Minh sympathizers. Pracheachon activities were kept under fairly close scrutiny, and Sihanouk let it be known that the Pracheachon operated under instructions from Hanoi rather than Peking, although neither capital accorded Pracheachon representatives any form of recognition. Pracheachon plots against the Sihanouk regime were publicized in much the same way as the transgressions of the CIA. In February, 1960, accompanied by both the Soviet and Chinese ambassadors on a visit to a dam site in the province of Svay Rieng, Sihanouk had claimed publicly that he had abundant proof (including Viet-Minh documents) that the Pracheachon was "working indefatigably for the Communist world and specifically to bring Cambodia under the heel of North Viet-Nam." [22]

In August, 1961, soon after his return from Geneva, Sihanouk took open action against the Pracheachon, although the form this action took indicated an attempt to repress by social ostracism rather than by actual physical measures. The Pracheachon had sought to raise certain issues for debate at the Twelfth National Congress, due to be held at the end of August. In order to highlight the apparent antinational outlook of the Pracheachon, Sihanouk decided to call a special congress on August 1 to deal with the issues involved, especially a scandal over misappropriation of public funds. The declared purpose of the congress was to draw attention to a group described by Sihanouk as "our local Communists," a group which had "done everything in its power to sow dissension in the bosom of the nation." [23] Sihanouk went out of his way to make "the Khmer Communists" the object of public scorn, but, as the congress progressed, it became evident that the Cambodian leader was primarily concerned lest the growth of political divisions, especially of a generational kind, reproduce the internecine conflict so evident in Laos. During August, Sihanouk commented frequently and dispairingly that Laos was moving inevitably toward Communism. He had no desire to see internal division within Cambodia offer the same fruitful field for intervention when, as he expected, the country would be bordered on the north by a Communist Laos.

It became clear that Sihanouk saw the Pracheachon as a symbol of the dissent expressed by those he described as youthful progressive intellectuals. While he treated the Pracheachon as such with open ridicule and contempt, he discussed more seriously the threat to national unity posed by the more ambitious young intellectuals. He complained that his efforts to give them positions of responsibility in the country and to advance their careers at the expense of older officials had been little appreciated. He pointed out, "I tried this experiment with a view to avoiding conflict between the new generation and the older—a conflict which would have struck a fatal blow at national unity which I was anxious to achieve and consolidate." [24] He expressed his disillusionment at the result of "this experiment," contending that the young intellectuals "want to torpedo our present regime and replace it with Communism." [25] Finally, he found it necessary to threaten that his party would not stand at the next elections, but would let the people choose whether they wished to return to a multiparty system or adopt Communism.

The special congress produced a popular reaction against the Pracheachon as sowers of national dissension, undermining the masses and the young, but Sihanouk refused to accede to requests to ban the party. It is apparent that he did not regard the organization as particularly dangerous and was willing to have it exist in a state of open proscription[26] so that he could capitalize on its alleged antinational role to deal with a more serious problem—the growing educated class of young men whose dissatisfaction with the governing system might undermine Cambodia's national unity, its greatest strength.

After the special congress, Sihanouk went on a tour of Kompong Cham Province. During a speech, he enumerated the evils of Communism, stressing its brutality and denial of individual liberty, and refuted what he claimed was Pracheachon propaganda suggesting that Communism meant a redistribution of the wealth of the rich among the poor. "In fact," he said, "the truth is quite different. Communism confiscates property but does not then distribute it to the poor. Confiscated private property becomes the property of the State and the poor remain as before, the poor." He explained the present recrudescence of Pracheachon activity as a result of "the victory recently gained by Communism in Laos." [27] This explanation also provides an exegesis of his own behavior in seeking to arouse popular opinion against the Pracheachon and sustain national unity in the face of his discontented progressive intellectuals.

At this stage, we begin to observe the beginnings of a modification of neutrality from a policy founded on equal balance to a policy that seeks to respond to a transformation of that balance in favor of one side. Sihanouk had no desire to give up Cambodia's independent status, but he recognized that the immediate threat came not from direct aggression but from internal division on the Laos model. He was prepared to face up to eventual Communist dominance, but he felt that Cambodia as a unified nation might survive despite the removal of Western countervailing power. In telling of his meeting with Cambodian students abroad who had been influenced by events in Laos, he said, "I set about showing these students that our present strength lies in our unity in a common ideal, a single political faith, and that I shall not hesitate when the time comes for me to yield to Communism to prepare our people and myself to become Communists to prevent the dispute of our unity and the shedding of blood." [28]

At the end of August, while the Geneva Conference on Laos continued its thus far fruitless deliberations, Sihanouk left Cambodia to attend the Belgrade meeting of nonaligned countries and the Sixteenth Session of the United Nations General Assembly. At both gatherings, Sihanouk sought an international guarantee for Cambodia's neutrality, which he hoped would be tied in with a general settlement for Laos. In this context, he urged upon the neutrals assembled in Belgrade the necessity of creating buffer zones in the areas most directly threatened by the confrontation of the two blocs. His formula, directly related to Cambodia's security needs, was as follows: "It is simply a matter of persuading the two blocs to admit the usefulness of a chain of countries, whose neutrality they would solemnly recognize and guarantee, in order to eliminate the risk of conflict, which is greatest in the case of common frontiers." [29] Sihanouk made the same point before the United Nations General Assembly, suggesting that the United Nations study the practical ways and means of neutralizing countries that wanted to be neutralized. He also made apparent his fear that Cambodia would find itself faced with a division similar to that of Laos or even South Viet-Nam, should bloc rivalry transport itself to his kingdom.

Neither in Belgrade nor in New York did Sihanouk find cause for optimism about his country's future. In a speech in Tokyo, on his way back to Cambodia, he publicly recognized that Cambodia's security could no longer be sustained by a balance that involved Western countervailing power. One section of this speech stood out because it acknowledged the transformation of Southeast Asia:

> The SEATO bastion exists no longer, except in the imagination of armchair strategists of the Western press. SEATO was remarkable for the organization of conferences which made platonic decisions or for combined military exercises which have never impressed anyone. Its performance in South Viet-Nam and Laos have been much less remarkable. It has proved that all it was able to do by pushing local governments into deeper commitment thereby bringing thunder down on their heads, was to hasten the disintegration of the countries it wishes to defend. The defeat of the Laotian tendency which had become accepted to become [sic] a bastion of the Free

World in Southeast Asia has signed SEATO's death warrant. The West should have understood that the best defense against Communism in Asia is not to oppose a military force against an inevitably superior military force.[30]

The Laotian crisis, and the related growing conflict in Viet-Nam, may be seen as a watershed in the development of Cambodian foreign policy. Internally there was no change; at the end of October, 1961, for example, public pressure against the Pracheachon was intensified when Sihanouk took part in a radio confrontation with the editor of a leftist newspaper. Sihanouk continued to warn of discord created by young intellectuals which could lead Cambodia to the same fate as Laos and Viet-Nam. He made it plain that the government intended to deal severely with those of Communist sympathy. In January, 1962, Sihanouk announced the arrest of fourteen members of the Pracheachon Party, including its leader, Non Suon.

Sihanouk was determined to prevent internal divisions that could undermine national unity, but there was growing evidence that Cambodia would have to bend its foreign policy before the prevailing wind rather than remain in the happy equilibrium sustained by an East-West balance of influence. For example, on January 16, 1962, when Sihanouk addressed the National Assembly about the problem of young intellectuals, he concluded his remarks by declaring himself resigned to Communist takeover, stating, "We will become Communists together, and our Union will be preserved." [31]

Sihanouk was able to forestall what he regarded as antinational opposition, but he had no control over external forces. Relations with his neighbors had continued to deteriorate. Cambodia and Thailand had broken diplomatic relations in October, 1961, and as a consequence Cambodia experienced increasing difficulties with the United States. On the other hand, the United States had not shown itself able to halt Communist success and, at the same time, the principal Communist power in Asia had maintained the appearance of amity toward Cambodia. Sihanouk saw no alternative but to bow to the inevitable, with the important reservation that he would seek by any means possible to try to preserve Cambodian independence. His growing pessimism was reflected in his remarks on the situation in South Viet-Nam:

> It is certain that the "free world" has lost there a most important battle. It is an inevitable disaster. This disaster cannot be changed into a victory, not even into a draw. It has been almost impossible to change the defeat of the pro-Western camp in Laos into a draw. All the more so, therefore, in South Viet-Nam, where things have gone too far along the road to disaster, is it unjustified to hope for even a re-establishment of the equilibrium which existed there a few years ago.[32]

7

The Demand for a Guarantee

In July, 1961, Sihanouk wrote that, once it accepted neutrality, Laos would move slowly but surely along the road to Communization.[1] After the announcement in June, 1962, of the agreement between the factions in Laos, an editorial in the authoritative weekly *Réalités cambodgiennes* informed its readers that nothing had happened in Laos to make Sihanouk alter his opinion.

The Laos settlement offered meager comfort to Cambodia.[2] It did little to encourage optimism about the continuation of American influence in Indochina as a counter to Communist advance. SEATO—the symbol of Western determination to retain that influence—took a hammering in the final agreements of the Geneva Conference. The Conference specifically forbade SEATO protection of Laos. The Laotian Government declared that it would not recognize the protection of any alliance—and specifically named SEATO—while the other signatories at Geneva undertook to respect that intention.[3] Equally significant was the fact that the Communists achieved the withdrawal of United States military support for its favored faction, without accepting international control of a kind that might obstruct the seizure of power.[4]

The outcome of the conference disturbed Sihanouk. However much he had been embroiled with the United States as a result of his neighbors' blandishments, its influence was of fundamental value in posing the countervailing power that sustained Cambodian neutrality. With the evident crumbling of the American position, not only in Laos but also in South Viet-Nam, Cambodia could foresee a return to the situation of 1954, but without the reassuring influence of the United States. It was therefore absolutely necessary to face up to the new balance of forces reflected in the Laos settlement. Sihanouk was in a favorable position to change his tack. He had enjoyed a happy association with the Chinese People's Republic, and had not experienced any special difficulties with the Hanoi regime, in spite of his denunciations of its control of the Pracheachon. Cambodia's increasing difficulties with South Viet-Nam and Thailand attracted the apparent sympathetic support of the Communist powers.[5] If Cambodia was to survive, it had to demonstrate that it was more useful to the interests of China to seek the preservation of Cambodia than to promote its disintegration through subversion of the kind that had been practiced in 1954, though this clearly would not be as easy a task in 1962.

Cambodia's security requirements were simple. Sihanouk wished to preserve his nation's territorial integrity. The difficulty was one of means. He decided to seek insulation and protection through great power guarantees. He apparently hoped that such guarantees would produce a balance of political forces that would automatically ensure territorial integrity. The Laos settlement had demonstrated that such a desirable balance no longer existed. A set of great power guarantees would be of some value, however, if they involved public commitments from those most likely to harbor ambitions that could be fulfilled only at Cambodia's expense.

The most likely to be ambitious on the Western side were Thailand and South Viet-Nam, although South Viet-Nam was clearly too involved in its internal problems to have much energy left to threaten Cambodia. Thailand would present a serious threat, but this could be neutralized by Communist backing. A greater anxiety, but not an immediate eventuality, was the prospect of a neutral or even pro-Communist Thailand, to which China might give free rein at Cambodia's expense.

From the Communist side, Sihanouk was most concerned about the intentions of North Viet-Nam, which in 1953–54 had sought to combine ideological motives with traditional Vietnamese aims. Because of the conclusions he drew from the Laos settlement and his view of the outcome of the conflict between North and South Viet-Nam, Sihanouk was most concerned by the prospect of a frontier in common with a Communist power which was also a traditional enemy. If North Viet-Nam could be brought to make a public commitment to respect Cambodia's independence and if, at the same time, the Chinese People's Republic could be involved in this arrangement, Cambodia would benefit from any restraining influence the Chinese might feel it in their own interests to exercise over North Viet-Nam. One could argue that such an arrangement to safeguard Cambodia's integrity might well be worked out informally without the necessity of a public stand. Sihanouk probably reasoned that public commitments would make the task of Cambodia's potential enemies more difficult, especially as Cambodia was much less ripe for the type of subversion that had been so successfully applied in South Viet-Nam. He was probably heartened in his endeavors by the stand the South Vietnamese National Liberation Front took after the Laos agreement: The Front called for the strict and positive neutrality of South Viet-Nam and announced that Cambodia, Laos, and South Viet-Nam should form a neutral zone in which each member state would enjoy full sovereignty.

On August 20, 1962, Sihanouk sent a message to all the governments that had taken part in the Geneva Conference on Laos except Thailand requesting that another international gathering be summoned to provide Cambodia with "the benefits of the arrangements for international protection which were granted to Laos." [6] This action drew a warm response from Communist countries and from France, but the United States, Britain, India, and Burma were not at all enthusiastic about the prospect of another conference. The Communists clearly had nothing to lose by accepting Sihanouk's proposal. Such an occasion could be exploited to belabor the United States with the misdeeds of its allies and even to take up the question of the neutralization of South Viet-Nam. Sihanouk was not disturbed by the thought that the occasion could be an unnecessary embarrassment to the United States Government. In order to get public commitments from his Communist neighbors, the United States would have to agree to participate in the conference.

Sihanouk reacted to the failure of his diplomatic initiative by threatening to revise his country's policy of neutrality and to ask China and the Soviet Union to send troops to protect Cambodia against its Western-aligned neighbors. On the face of it, Cambodia was seeking a guarantee against the evil intentions of South Viet-Nam and Thailand. An alleged incursion by Thai soldiers on August 11 provided justification for Sihanouk's appeal for international assistance. It would not have been politic to call publicly on China and the Soviet Union to defend Cambodia against the ambitions of North Viet-Nam. Sihanouk was eager to secure protection from Peking against North Viet-Nam, but to this end it was necessary to present his demands in terms of protection against the allies of the United States. Although Sihanouk sought not much more than the presence of the United States to give the conference a genuine great power quality, he was asking too much to expect that country to lean on its allies in public, if only for effect, as well as to let itself serve as a convenient object of Communist abuse. Sihanouk acknowledged this difficulty, pointing out somewhat sarcastically that he was well aware of the embarrassing position in which the nations of the "free world" would find themselves at a conference convened to discuss a situation due solely to their intervention in the internal affairs of the Indochinese Peninsula and to the aggressive activities of their satellites. He said that their reluctance to appear in the role of the guilty party accounted, therefore, for their hesitation in approving his proposal.[7]

Having failed in his attempt to obtain a guarantee by conference, Sihanouk tried a different approach. He announced that his government did not attach overriding importance to the means adopted to enforce the guarantees in question. He expressed his readiness to accept the guarantees contained in the agreement on Laos, which provided for an immediate reconvening of the Geneva Conference whenever an act of aggression was confirmed. He then proposed that, in view of the refusal of the American Government to allow its delegates to sit at a conference table with representatives of the Communist Chinese Government, the agreement suggested (on the Laotian pattern) should be signed in the respective capitals of the interested parties. Finally, Sihanouk suggested that if this alternative proved unworkable, he would be prepared to content himself with an official declaration from the prospective participants in the conference, provided such a declaration effectively protected his country's neutrality and territorial integrity. By that he meant that the declaration should contain an agreement to come to Cambodia's assistance in the event of an unprovoked attack on its territory.

All Sihanouk's demands were founded on the ostensible premise that Cambodia's security was being threatened only by Thailand and South Viet-Nam. He stated openly that if all his reasonable alternatives were rejected, he would be forced to reconsider his country's foreign policy and ask China and the Soviet Union to provide troops, because Cambodia's armed strength was insufficient to face up to a concerted attack on two fronts.

On November 5, Sihanouk announced that certain Western governments were showing little enthusiasm for the document he had suggested. Nothing came of this initiative, and Sihanouk seemed content to let the matter rest. On November 26, he left Phnom Penh on a tour of Asian capitals beginning with Djakarta, and the question of a guarantee or some form of protective arrangement for Cambodia lapsed for the time being. One can only conjecture over Sihanouk's loss of enthusiasm. The Western powers certainly seemed unwilling to support his proposals, and Sihanouk himself probably had second thoughts about the efficacy of simple declarations of intent. The Sino-Indian border war dominated Asian international political life toward the end of 1962, and it is possible that the impact of this dramatic event so overshadowed Sihanouk's initiatives that he felt it politic to drop the question of a guarantee for the time being. He did not return to the subject of a guarantee or a conference until almost a year later, when he interpreted the fall of the Diem regime in South Viet-Nam as a sign that Cambodia would shortly be sharing her eastern border with a reunited Communist Viet-Nam.

Accommodation to China

Many benefits to Cambodia had accrued from its association with the Chinese People's Republic, including aid allocations for the construction of industrial plants. Association with China seemed to restrain left-wing forces within Cambodia as well as the Chinese minority. It offered the prospect of control over North Vietnamese ambitions, which in 1953–54 the Hanoi regime had prosecuted at Cambodia's expense. It also served to ward off what in Cambodia were regarded as the predatory aims of Thailand and South Viet-Nam. Cambodia had good reason not to risk losing the good will China had manifested in December, 1960, when it agreed to sign the Treaty of Friendship and Nonaggression with Cambodia.[8] Even before the treaty, Cambodia scrupulously avoided any association that might lead to friction with Peking. Late in 1959, Sihanouk received an invitation from Malaysian Prime Minister Tunku Abdul Rahman to discuss the formation of a Southeast Asian Friendship and Economic Treaty. The Philippines and Thailand—both members of SEATO—were among those who also received invitations. Sihanouk rejected the idea out of hand, explaining that to join in the formation of an organization known to be favored by two members of SEATO and sponsored by the anti-Communist government of Malaysia would seem to be "temerarious." The official comment was, "We value our hard-won independence too highly to throw it away in some ill-considered move which would justifiably anger the Communist powers." [9]

After the crisis in Laos in 1960 and the establishment of the National Liberation Front in South Viet-Nam at the end of the year,[10] Cambodia's association with Communist China became increasingly important as a national insurance policy. Following the disappointment of the Laos Conference and the failure of Cambodia's attempt to secure an international guarantee, Cambodia drew even closer to Communist China. Striking evidence of this diplomatic alignment was demonstrated at the time of the Sino-Indian Border War, whose decisive outcome impressed Phnom Penh.

Sihanouk found himself reluctantly involved in the settlement that followed the border conflict. With some embarrassment, he received an invitation from the Prime Minister of Ceylon, Mrs. Bandaranaike, to participate in a conference of neutrals to consider the Sino-Indian War and ways to achieve a peaceful settlement of that conflict at Colombo, in December, 1962. The invitation accorded him the international distinction he felt he deserved, but Sihanouk would have preferred, if possible, to avoid that particular honor. It presented a serious dilemma. There was the chilling prospect that such a meeting might transform itself into an arbitration tribunal that could be distinctly offensive to China. The risk certainly outweighed any personal glory that might accrue from participation in a conference at which neither of the actual belligerents was to be represented.[11]

The Cambodian position at Colombo was to avoid involvement in any collective decision to which the Chinese might object. Sihanouk had no inclination to upset Cambodia's happy association with Peking for the sake of temporary glory in Colombo.[12] Like Burma's Premier Ne Win, who was equally concerned not to provoke the Chinese Government, Sihanouk was careful to dissociate himself from any positive set of proposals for resolving the conflict. He tried, though not too successfully, to direct the conference along the path of conciliation. He tried also to avoid any suggestion of arbitration, but recommended that the conference should devote itself to devising a means of inducing China and India to meet as friends without prior commitment on either side. This argument met with approval in Peking and also appeared to cause no great consternation in New Delhi, where Cambodian anxieties seemed to be appreciated. During a visit to India in February, 1963, Sihanouk proclaimed his sympathy for what he described as Cambodia's spiritual fatherland. While the Cambodian press referred to India as a sister nation, it also stressed that "friendship with China is for us as oxygen is to a diver." From New Delhi, Sihanouk journeyed to Peking, where political expediency took precedence over cultural affinity. The Chinese Government rewarded Sihanouk's caution at Colombo with warm praise. At one of many banquets, Chairman Liu Shao-chi described Cambodia's friendship as "most precious." [13]

When Liu Shao-chi paid a return visit to Cambodia in May, 1963, Sihanouk used the occasion to assure his guest of Cambodia's good will, and remarked on the total absence of chauvinism in Communist China's relations with all countries. Whatever the precise motive behind this statement—whether intended as an attempt at ingratiation or even as an expression of concern about the future—it was warmly welcomed in Peking.[14]

Concern over Chinese sensitivity prompted an incident that marked Cambodia's entry into the politics of international sports. Differences with the International Amateur Athletic Federation prompted the Cambodian Amateur Athletic Federation to withdraw from that body in April, 1963, and to cancel the Third Southeast Asian Peninsula Games, scheduled to be held in Phnom Penh. This decision arose out of the hotly disputed 1962 Asian Games held in Djakarta, from which Nationalist China and Israel were deliberately excluded. Cambodia refused to join in condemning Indonesia. The Cambodian Government enjoys normal diplomatic relations with Israel, and the most plausible explanation for Cambodia's behavior was its unwillingness to condemn the exclusion of Nationalist China from the Djakarta games, an action that would hardly have endeared Cambodia to Communist China. The Chinese Physical Culture and Sports Commission and the All-China Athletic Federation supported Cambodia's "just action." In November, 1963, Cambodia sent a team to participate in the Games of the New Emerging Forces, held in Djakarta, an action Communist China regarded with benevolence.

Cambodia moved even closer to China as a result of the growing Sino-Soviet dispute. In September, 1962, Cambodia had entered into diplomatic relations with Albania, thus suggesting a preference between China and the Soviet Union. The successful negotiation of the partial nuclear-test-ban treaty in July, 1963, between the United States, Britain, and the Soviet Union forced Cambodia farther away from a position of formal neutrality. The almost universal adherence to the treaty by Communist and non-Communist states gave Cambodia no opportunity to adopt a nonaligned position. The Chinese People's Republic, echoed by Albania, publicly denounced the accord as "a huge deceit" and as "a capitulation before the American imperialists." [15] The Cambodian Government was faced with a unique situation from which it was impossible to contract out. In view of the value of its relationship with China, Cambodia decided to adopt the Chinese stand. It not only refused to adhere to the test-ban treaty, but also denounced it, in the same vein as the Chinese, as a "bargain of dupes and a demogogic act." Sihanouk also echoed China's counterproposal for a world conference of heads of government on general disarmament.[16]

The significance Sihanouk attached to his country's association with the Chinese People's Republic was apparent in his justification of Cambodia's position on the test-ban treaty. "All things considered," he pointed out, "we prefer after all to be isolated *with* China rather than *against* China, which is the only country ready to fight at our side for our survival if this were directly threatened." [17] Sihanouk's action on the test-ban treaty was logical in terms of Cambodia's recognition of China's power and position in Asia and in the light of Cambodia's expectation that this power could be interposed along the border with Viet-Nam. The rationale for Cambodian behavior in relation to China was outlined in an article in *Cambodian Commentary*, then an official English-language publication of the Cambodian Government. The article asserted that "all Asian leaders are certainly aware that the interlude in their history marked by European intervention in Asian affairs is drawing to a close and the time is fast approaching when they will be faced with that recurrent factor; a resurgent China with which they will have to come to terms as best they may." [18]

The Cambodian Government regarded accommodation of China as a necessary posture toward a country it believed was certain to dominate Asia in the future and which it needed for protection against the traditional threats from Thailand and Viet-Nam. While Sihanouk seemed to feel greatest concern over the prospect of a reunited Viet-Nam under the control of the regime in Hanoi, he drew no distinction between Communist or non-Communist Vietnamese. He had written: "Whether he is called Gia Long, Ho Chi Minh or Ngo Dinh Diem, no Annamite (or Vietnamese) will sleep peacefully until he has succeeded in pushing Cambodia toward annihilation, having made it first go through the stages of slavery." [19] He was certain by the end of 1963, as he entitled an article, that "South Viet-Nam's Fate Appears Sealed." [20] In a press interview in mid-1963, Sihanouk admitted that Cambodia was on friendly terms with North Viet-Nam because it was a "strong power." He continued, "But we could not be friendly with North Viet-Nam unless South Viet-Nam stood between our countries as it does now." [21] The coup in South Viet-Nam that removed the Diem regime in November, 1963, convinced Sihanouk that he ought to prepare for the worst. He reacted by renewing his demand for an international conference that would provide Cambodia with an effective guarantee of its neutrality.

The Crisis of November, 1963

During 1963, Cambodia's relations with Thailand remained at a low level, but relations with South Viet-Nam had become increasingly difficult. Cambodian villages along the border with South Viet-Nam were being hurt by the South Vietnamese policy of pursuing across the border the insurgent Viet-Cong. At the same time, the repression of the South Vietnamese Buddhists by the Diem regime hardened attitudes even further in Phnom Penh. At the end of August, 1963, the Cambodian Government broke off diplomatic relations with South Viet-Nam, "in view of the countless crimes the latter government has been ceaselessly perpetuating for years against the Khmer people of Cambodia, the Khmer community of Kampuchea Krom, and Buddhism." [22]

In the following months, the Khmer Serai—allegedly led by Son Ngoc Thanh and supported by the South Vietnamese Government and the CIA—began to broadcast to Cambodia. The tenor of these transmissions was personally insulting to Sihanouk. He became extremely alarmed and even obsessed at the continuation of the broadcasts, which made him feel extremely insecure, and he needed little convincing that agents of the United States were again working to overthrow him.

At the beginning of November, 1963, South Vietnamese President Ngo Dinh Diem was removed from office by a coup that resulted in his death. Sihanouk saw the hand of the United States in the overthrow of Diem. While he had no love for Diem, he was deeply concerned that the United States could remove such an indomitable figure from the Southeast Asian scene.[23] He was disturbed at the political consequences of the coup and at the possibility of being the next victim. In July, 1962, Sihanouk had committed himself in print to the belief that the Americans could be assured of the determination of the local government in South Viet-Nam to struggle to the death against the Viet-Minh, despite the situation there. At the same time, however, he had expressed fears about the day Viet-Nam would be unified, "with Ho Chi Minh at our door." [24] He was undoubtedly alarmed that the overthrow of Diem might also be the signal for Viet-Cong success. He had admitted less than two months previously, "I foresee perfectly well the collapse of an independent and neutral Cambodia after the complete triumph of Communism in Laos and South Viet-Nam." [25]

Visibly shaken by Diem's death, Sihanouk saw himself confronted by two equally unattractive alternatives: either the collapse of the Western position in South Viet-Nam, followed by unification of the country on Communist terms, or the duplication of American tactics in Cambodia and his own assassination to install a regime more to U.S. liking. The measures he adopted subsequently can be construed as attempts to cover all possibilities. After about November 5, Sihanouk began a three-week period of speech-making, and, at the end of that time, he had dramatically transformed Cambodia's relationship with the United States. At the outset, he threatened to reject all American aid if the Khmer Serai radio stations did not cease their transmissions. Sihanouk had been reconsidering the value of American assistance for some time, because he felt that it had a corrupting influence on the Khmer people, preventing them from becoming self-reliant. On his visit to Peking early in 1963, the Chinese had expressed concern about the growing American presence in Cambodia. On November 19, Sihanouk called a special National Congress before which he presented a captured member of the Khmer Serai who claimed that the CIA had provided ammunition and funds for the movement. Sihanouk then called for the immediate withdrawal of United States military, economic, and cultural aid to Cambodia because of American support for the Khmer Serai. The Congress authorized the renunciation of aid as Sihanouk recommended, and on the following day the decision was communicated to Washington.

The removal of the American presence was intended to reduce

its potential for interference in Cambodia's internal affairs. It was also intended to produce an evocative response by the younger generation, which normally expressed its left-wing ideas in anti-American form. The Chinese responded most favorably to the Cambodian action, issuing a strong statement of support that promised assistance in the event of armed invasion instigated by the United States and its allies. During this same period, Sihanouk moved to break the Chinese minority's stranglehold on the economy by nationalizing foreign trade and the banks.

Two days after the decision to terminate American aid—which had totaled more than $350 million since 1955—Sihanouk revived his demand for a conference to guarantee Cambodia's neutrality. The main task of such a conference, he felt, would be to provide the International Control Commission with the staff and equipment to ensure Cambodia's true neutrality. Sihanouk may have hoped to capitalize on Western alarm about his rejection of American aid to gain acceptance of his demand for a conference, but no Western response was forthcoming. The American position was that, since Cambodia believed that its main threat came from Thailand and South Viet-Nam, direct negotiations with these countries, rather than an international conference, would be the most suitable way of resolving difficulties. The United States was determined not to permit the Cambodian issue to be exploited to its disadvantage. Britain agreed in principle on the need to guarantee Cambodian neutrality, "but did not believe that a large conference, which inevitably would have taken up the situation in Laos and South Viet-Nam, was the practical way to settle border problems." [26] France and Communist China, which advocated neutralization as the political solution for the Viet-Nam crisis, supported the idea of a conference.

Sihanouk continued to press for a conference, but on a different basis. On November 24, he announced that Cambodia's last recourse was to appeal to the 1954 Geneva Conference. The Cambodian Foreign Minister, Huot Sambath, then sent a message to the co-chairmen requesting that the nine powers reconvene to consider the threat to his country's neutrality.[27] Meanwhile, Cambodian-American relations went from bad to worse. On December 9, Radio Phnom Penh commented that the Cambodian people had heard with joy of the deaths of Sarit, Diem, and "the big boss of these aggressors."[28] The American Government instructed its ambassador to Cambodia to seek an explanation for that distasteful reference to the recent assassination of President Kennedy. The Cambodian Government dismissed the incident as a misunderstanding, but the U. S. State Department described the explanation as "unsatisfactory."[29] The outcome of this sordid affair was the Cambodian decision to withdraw its embassy staffs from the United States and Britain, but without formally breaking off diplomatic relations.

By this time, Sihanouk's behavior was beyond rational analysis in the United States. On January 11, in a speech to a Buddhist Congress, he declared his willingness to accept any aid that the United States wanted to give, but only if it was offered without conditions. Sihanouk even extended the deadline for the departure of United States military and economic advisers. The State Department, however, was sick to death of Sihanouk's erratic temperament and stipulated that any resumption of aid would have to be preceded by a formal agreement. Congressional scrutiny of aid programs at that time would have created great difficulty in restoring aid, even if the U. S. Government had been willing to do so. Washington felt that Sihanouk should stew in his own juice, particularly since it saw the whole prolonged crisis as part of Sihanouk's efforts to force the U. S. Government to agree to an international conference. One American official was reported as saying: "We cannot go into a conference where we appear to be one of the trespassers of the indictment."[30]

A British Initiative

British Foreign Secretary R. A. Butler indicated in November, 1963, that he was prepared to consider ways and means to safeguard Cambodian neutrality. The Cambodian Government responded by dispatching three documents. The first was a declaration of its own neutrality, the second was a declaration of respect for its neutrality to be signed by the other participants of the Laos Conference, and the third was a protocol relating to the second. Article 2 of the declaration of respect for Cambodia's neutrality involved substantial obligations for the signatories. It began, for example, by assuming that the signatories would "neither commit nor permit in any way any act, directly or indirectly, against the sovereignty, independence, neutrality, and territorial integrity of the Kingdom of Cambodia, nor will it participate in any way in any act of this nature." Perhaps even more significant than such an onerous commitment were the clear references to the two Viet-Nams; the proposals were predicated on the continuing division of Cambodia's traditional enemy.[31]

The search for a guarantee now centered on the exchange with the British Foreign Secretary. Butler replied on January 9, 1964, and referred to an earlier communication in which his government had agreed to support in principle the Cambodian demand for a conference. He foresaw certain difficulties arising from the question of participation unless there was a clear understanding on the nature of the agreement to be adopted at such a conference. He then put forward an alternative declaration and protocol that would have committed the governments concerned to recognize, respect, and observe the sovereignty, independence, neutrality, and territorial integrity of Cambodia. It would also have authorized the International Control Commission to supervise the working of the accord. According to Butler, Sihanouk welcomed these drafts.[32]

The dialogue was interrupted on January 21 by a Soviet proposal that a fourteen-nation conference, to be attended by the United States, should take place the following April. As co-chairman of the Geneva Conference on Indochina, Britain was to be a joint sponsor of such a meeting. This proposal caused the British Government acute embarrassment. While, on the one hand, they

did not wish to appear to be opposed to a conference, they felt it
necessary to establish in advance a form of agreement that would
be acceptable to the United States as well as to Cambodia. Clearly,
the United States would not be willing to commit itself to a meeting in which its role in South Viet-Nam would be criticized by
Communist participants and also by France, which had proposed
a vague plan for neutralization to include Viet-Nam. When Butler
wrote again to Sihanouk on January 28, he sought to dissuade
him from the idea of a conference. He referred to a previous offer
by Malaysian Prime Minister Tunku Abdul Rahman to try to arrange a meeting between Cambodia, Thailand, and South Viet-
Nam. Butler pointed out that such a meeting would serve Cambodia's purpose better than an international conference. He
pointed out that if Britain accepted the demand of the Soviet co-
chairman, the result would be contrary to what both Britain and
Cambodia desired, since the United States was not willing to go
to the conference table before the terms of reference of such a
conference were clearly established.

Sihanouk replied at the beginning of February that he approved without modification the British draft agreement. He did
not, however, believe that such a conference should be subordi-
nated to a meeting between Thais, South Vietnamese, and Cambodians. He thought precious time would be lost in waiting for
neighbors to decide on a meeting that basically they did not
want. He expressed a lack of understanding of the American attitude to a conference. He stated that his patience had limits and
threatened to break off diplomatic relations with the United
States if, by the end of May, it still wished to obstruct a project
that was of vital importance to Cambodia. Two weeks later, Sihanouk increased his threat by warning that he would sign a
military pact with Communist China and North Viet-Nam if the
United States did not accept the Cambodian neutralization plan
by May. He also threatened to recognize the Hanoi regime as
the sole government for Viet-Nam, claiming it had recognized
the integrity of Cambodia and did not contest the sovereignty of

its off-shore islands.[33] Sihanouk's ultimatum lends itself to interpretation as a crude attempt at blackmail. However crude his methods, his evaluation of his country's security problems was rather sophisticated. His frank admission of the real threat to Cambodia indicated that he was attempting to use the presence of the United States and its allies at a conference to obtain a public commitment from powers whose ambitions were his greatest concern. A week after his ultimatum he announced:

> Quite frankly, it is not in our interests to deal with the West, which represents the present but not the future. In ten years' time, there will probably be in Thailand, which always responds to the dominant wind, a pro-Chinese neutralist government, and South Viet-Nam will certainly be governed by Ho Chi Minh or his successor. Our interests are served by dealing with the camp that one day will dominate the whole of Asia—and by coming to terms before its victory—in order to obtain the best terms possible.[34]

Another Dialogue

Sihanouk had recognized the limitations placed on the freedom of the British Government in seeking to arrange a conference. He decided, therefore, to make a direct approach to the United States, suggesting that the British draft text should serve as the basis for discussions for a four-power conference to be attended by the United States, Thailand, South Viet-Nam, and Cambodia. Such a conference would agree to respect Cambodia's neutrality and its existing frontiers.

On March 3, Cambodian Foreign Minister Huot Sambath sent a formal note to Secretary of State Dean Rusk,[35] the form of the note indicating that Cambodia regarded the four-power conference as a means to arm itself diplomatically in seeking similar guarantees from North Viet-Nam and China. Sambath suggested that the declaration, if signed by the four countries, would then be submitted to the other countries that had attended the Geneva Conference on Laos. The State Department responded with proposals it wished to have considered at the conference. This alternative plan was supposedly designed to reassure America's allies that it would not desert them in Phnom Penh and to encourage them to attend the conference themselves. In any event, the American counterproposals prevented the holding of the conference. Some claim that they served as a pretext for the Cambodians to cancel the conference once they realized that the Thais would not come to Phnom Penh under any circumstances. The point at issue was a suggestion in the American draft protocol that mixed delimitation commissions be established to determine the frontier between Cambodia and Thailand and between Cambodia and South Viet-Nam. The corresponding section in the Cambodian draft had sought to rely on demarcations that had been made in the past by the French.

Penn Nouth, a former Prime Minister and trusted adviser of Sihanouk, objected to the American counterproposals because the Cambodian initiative had established the Butler draft as the only basis for discussion. He also read malicious intent in the suggestion concerning delimitation of frontiers, seeing this as a means of challenging Cambodia's frontiers and as an opportunity for the Thais to contest the decision of the International Court of Justice on the Prah Vihar Temple. In a second letter to Dean Rusk, Penn Nouth claimed that the United States had violated an informal agreement reached between himself and the U. S. Ambassador in Phnom Penh and that, because of the American position on the question of frontiers, there was no point in pursuing the matter of a four-power conference.[36]

On March 9, Sihanouk accused the United States of plotting to partition Cambodia and threatened to negotiate alliances with North Viet-Nam and the Pathet Lao. On March 10, a Cambodian military mission, led by Army Commander-in-Chief Lon Nol, left for Peking and Moscow with an authorization to purchase arms. The Cambodian Government had contemplated this mission for some time, but its timing was a pointed gesture. More drastic measures followed. On March 11, a Phnom Penh crowd mobilized by the Ministry of Information stormed and sacked the American and British embassies and wrecked the U. S. Information Library and the British Council. Sihanouk himself had given the order for the demonstration after a long discussion with his advisers on how to demonstrate Cambodian annoyance at what was regarded as a maneuver to postpone the conference indefinitely. What Sihanouk had planned as a demonstration turned into a riot. He probably suffered some remorse when it was suggested that he was merely following the example of Sukarno in inspiring a demonstration of petty spite.

The British Government received a note from the Cambodian Foreign Ministry expressing regret at the damage to the embassy in Phnom Penh and giving assurance that compensation would be paid. At the same time, Butler received a message from Sihanouk stating that Cambodia would not attend a conference on his country's neutrality unless it took place within a week. The following day, March 18, South Vietnamese leader General Nguyên Khanh announced that a delegation from Saigon would go to Phnom Penh to discuss border problems.[37] At the same time, Sihanouk canceled plans to send a delegation to Hanoi to conclude a frontier agreement. These events seemed to introduce considerable flexibility into what had appeared to be a rigid and hopeless situation. It suggested that Sihanouk was prepared to leave the options open, rather than commit himself irrevocably to the Communist side. It also indicated that the United States, in urging General Khanh to negotiate, had seen through Cambodian abuse to Cambodian anxieties. For at the same time that there had been a prospect of a four-power conference, the Hanoi regime had indicated that the border problem between Cambodia and South Viet-Nam ought to be settled between the Cambodian Government and the National Liberation Front, and fear of antagonizing the likely victors in the Viet-Nam conflict probably played a part in Sihanouk's decision not to proceed with the meeting. Now, however, he seemed willing to confer with the representatives of the South Vietnamese Government. On March 20, when South Vietnamese forces chasing retreating Viet-Cong attacked the Cambodian village of Chantrea, leaving seventeen dead and thirteen wounded, Sihanouk refused to see the South Vietnamese delegation which had arrived in Phnom Penh the preceding day. The Saigon Government admitted responsibility and offered to pay compensation for the victims of the attack, and Sihanouk seemed touched by the expressions of regret from General Huynh, who led the delegation to Phnom Penh, but he would not proceed with the arranged discussions. He announced that common problems would be best resolved in the context of a Geneva-type conference.[38]

Sihanouk then offered to take up negotiations with South Viet-Nam and to send a delegation to Saigon if the co-chairmen would establish a date for convening a Geneva conference. The nature of this offer suggests that, even if the incident at Chantrea had not occurred, a settlement with South Viet-Nam would still have been conditional on a Geneva conference. In a speech made in Chantrea just after the incident, Sihanouk again referred to the imminence of the defeat of the Saigon Government, but at the same time he spoke of the problems that were likely to arise over Cambodia's frontiers in the future if the whole question were not settled immediately. In spite of his periodic claim that the government of North Viet-Nam was willing to sign a nonaggression pact and a frontier agreement, Sihanouk clearly did not place much reliance on this alternative.

8

Blocked Roads to Geneva

At the end of March, 1964, Sihanouk was interviewed by a reporter from *Time* who asked why he was so insistent on an international guarantee of neutrality. Sihanouk replied: "Suppose one day your camp is defeated. I apologize, but it is my conviction it will be. If I have nothing to show that we are a legally neutralist [*sic*] country with legal acceptance by an international conference, how can we survive? I don't trust the Communists too much. No. No. But recognition is much better than not having it."[1]

Sihanouk did not have his way. The British Government rejected the Soviet proposal for a conference to be held in April, pointing out that it was impossible to ensure the attendance of some of the fourteen nations who would have to be invited. As an alternative, it again proposed a four-power conference between Cambodia, the United States, South Viet-Nam, and Thailand.[2] Sihanouk responded by asserting that a four-power conference was out of the question because the Thais had refused to attend. He then accused the British Government of deliberately, hypocritically, and with Machiavellian intent sabotaging "our Geneva Conference."

The wrecking of the American and British embassies in Phnom Penh in March had seemed to mark the end of Sihanouk's patience with the Western powers. The British note that followed made it quite clear that little progress could be made toward convening the type of conference that would satisfy Sihanouk's requirements. Western diplomatic circles were concerned that Sihanouk, who had set another time limit for a conference, might engage in further volatile action. The furor over a conference to recognize Cambodia's neutrality had gone on for four months, and an earth-shattering climax was expected. However, to quote a correspondent, "Prince Sihanouk turned off the Cambodian crisis quite effortlessly, as if it were a tap." [3] Sihanouk had announced previously that, if a Geneva conference were not convened by his deadline, he would invite the Chinese to build two jet air bases in his country and would travel to Peking and Hanoi to establish more formal relations and frontier agreements with the North Vietnamese Government and the Pathet Lao. Now he seemed content to postpone action until he had returned from a visit to France in June, when he was to meet President de Gaulle. De Gaulle had advised Sihanouk to be patient and had shown himself very sympathetic to Sihanouk's difficulties. There was no indication, however, that de Gaulle would be able to grant Sihanouk's request for a conference. Circumstances had not changed in Southeast Asia.[4] One can only suggest that Sihanouk's decision to take a less active stance followed from a recognition of the very limited prospects of holding a conference.

Sihanouk's objective for Cambodia did not waver. At the end of June, during his visit to Paris, he addressed the Faculty of Law at the University of Paris, where he revealed his political testament. He informed his audience that he regarded himself essentially as a pragmatist. He had no doctrine to guide his conduct of his country's foreign affairs, but dealt with problems on a day-to-day basis. He abided by a simple rule of conduct: "to assume by all means imaginable the continued existence of my country and its independence and territorial integrity." [5] Sihanouk elaborated this theme as he described the broad lines of his foreign policy. The most important criterion was total independence in relation to foreign countries, "whoever they may be." He also expressed a determined desire not to permit "expansionist neighbors to impair the slightest piece of the national domain." When he insisted on keeping, at any cost, Cambodia for Cambodians in all its moral and physical integrity, he clearly viewed the prospect of a Communist victory in Southeast Asia with the utmost apprehension. He continued: "If our region must one day be submerged by Communism, we would wish that it be China and not another socialist country [which could only be North Viet-Nam] that takes control of our country, because we know that she understands us and that she will maintain . . . our territorial integrity. It goes without saying that we shall try, right up to the end, not to be anyone's satellite."

Sihanouk made it clear that he looked to the establishment of a traditional suzerain-subject relationship with China, which would be based on formal deference rather than subjugation. He recognized that the day would come when the socialist world would be able to "impose its lot," [6] but he foresaw continuing change in the structure of Asian Communism and even friction among its national adherents. His concern was to provide Cambodia with a breathing space during which Communist evolution would continue, and so permit the establishment of relationships based on mutual interest rather than ideological affinity. In this respect, Sihanouk apparently expected that his country would be the beneficiary of natural friction between China and Viet-Nam.[7] Meanwhile, he would avoid by all means possible any action that might antagonize the Chinese Government.[8]

Sihanouk saw only two options: either the neutralization of the three non-Communist countries in Indochina, or the pursuit of a war that would be unable to prevent Communization and would risk a generalized conflagration in the region. He criticized the American involvement in Viet-Nam as tactical folly that would only promote the spread of Communism. He expressed his annoyance at the American lack of comprehension that the differences between them were not based on varying attitudes toward Communism, but on the means to avoid the establishment of Communism throughout Indochina. He concluded with the perceptive argument that although the Communist countries accepted for the time being the neutralization of Cambodia, Laos, and South Viet-Nam, there was no guarantee that their position would not alter in the future. Such was indeed the case in South Viet-Nam after a series of Viet-Cong successes.

Sihanouk's visit to Paris confirmed an increasing association with France. In January, 1964, French Minister of Defense Pierre Messmer had journeyed to Phnom Penh to offer military assistance, including aircraft and tanks. Now, as a result of Sihanouk's meeting with President de Gaulle, France offered Cambodia credits equal to 160 million francs.[9] While such aid was both valuable and welcome, Sihanouk still insisted that the key to Cambodia's future was a conference to guarantee his country's neutrality. He continued to direct his energies to that objective. He saw no future in direct contact with the West and its allies. Relations with South Viet-Nam and the United States had deteriorated after a border penetration in May, and Cambodia had asked the United Nations Security Council to consider charges of aggression against both South Viet-Nam and the United States.

Mission to Peking

Sihanouk had made little, if any, progress toward convening a conference. The situation in Indochina, and especially in South Viet-Nam, was not static, and the prospect of sharing a common border with a reunited Communist Viet-Nam seemed to be increasing daily. During the previous March, Sihanouk had approached the North Vietnamese regime, hoping to persuade North Viet-Nam to recognize Cambodia's frontier with South Viet-Nam. This effort was not successful. While in Paris in June, he had held conversations with Vietnamese exiles, who supported the idea of a neutral Viet-Nam.[10] These discussions may have encouraged a second approach to North Viet-Nam. He intensified his efforts to court favor with Hanoi in August, when the United States began retaliatory attacks for the Gulf of Tonkin incident, in which North Vietnamese torpedo boats had fired on the warships of the Seventh Fleet. Sihanouk sent a telegram to Ho Chi Minh, condemning what he described as United States armed aggression against the Democratic Republic of Viet-Nam, and expressing his firm support for the Vietnamese people's courageous struggle against aggression.[11]

On a state visit to Peking in late September, Sihanouk gained offers of Chinese support in the event of armed aggression by "U.S. imperialism and its lackeys" and vague promises of military aid. But the primary objective of his visit was to persuade the Communist Vietnamese to commit themselves in writing to respect Cambodia's territorial integrity. He envisaged a formal recognition of frontiers, which China would then endorse and guarantee in the form of a defense pact. He had come to the agonizing decision that only by a formal approach to the Communist powers could he assure his country's future. He had revealed his state of mind in a letter to President de Gaulle the previous April in which he said:

> I must take into account the very precarious position of the present Saigon Government and it is difficult for me to mortgage the future unless an accord with the present Government of South Viet-Nam is rapidly sanctioned by the Geneva Conference. In effect, I cannot risk to see the National Liberation Front, which has a good chance of taking power in several months or several years, repudiate a treaty concluded with its adversary and which has not international sanction.[12]

This letter was written soon after Prince Sihanouk had announced that negotiations with South Viet-Nam were conditional upon the convening of a Geneva conference. Without the prospect of a conference, he felt it more politic to try to deal with the North Vietnamese, whom he regarded as the likely victors in the conflict in Viet-Nam.

In Peking, Sihanouk met with North Vietnamese Premier Pham

Van Dong, Foreign Minister Xuan Thuy, Prince Souvanna Phong of the Pathet Lao, and representatives of the South Vietnamese National Liberation Front.[13] Difficulties soon arose when Pham Van Dong pointed out that the National Liberation Front enjoyed competence on the question of Cambodia's frontiers with South Viet-Nam. The prospect of an accord with the National Liberation Front gave Sihanouk cause for apprehension. Recognition of this movement would infuriate the Saigon regime. He had to live side by side with the South Vietnamese Government, which had the power to retaliate against Cambodia. Sihanouk expressed his concern that South Viet-Nam could close the Mekong River and establish a partial economic blockade of Cambodia.[14] As Sihanouk continued his talk with the North Vietnamese Premier, he discovered a lack of enthusiasm about satisfying Cambodia's demands. Indeed, when Sihanouk pointed out the security risks for Cambodia involved in the type of recognition required by the Communists, Pham Van Dong replied that if such was the case, then his side was prepared to wait.[15] He implied that it would be up to the Communists, not Cambodia, to suggest terms in the future. Sihanouk received little comfort from the Chinese, who allegedly told him that it would serve his interests better to stay neutral than to become more closely aligned with the Communist powers.

Rejected in Peking, Sihanouk returned to Phnom Penh, where he announced that he had come to an agreement with North Viet-Nam and the National Liberation Front on the border question. He was careful to add that they had not signed a formal accord. His estimates of the time it would take the Communists to achieve victory ranged from several months to several years, and he was not entirely confident of an early outcome of the war in South Viet-Nam. The continuing incidents along the border with South Viet-Nam and the periodic bombing of Cambodian villages gave him cause for concern about the likely consequences of conceding formal recognition to North Viet-Nam and the National Liberation Front. Sihanouk's only hope for a guarantee was to secure the approval of all parties to the Vietnamese conflict—the potential losers as well as the potential victors.

Sihanouk was now reaping the bitter fruits of neutrality. Initially, he had based Cambodia's neutrality on a rough equilibrium of forces that made possible an independent posture. Circumstances now favored the Communists, but, because the outcome of events in Viet-Nam was still undetermined, Sihanouk had to seek the approval of both sides to sustain his country's position. Naturally, there was no automatic coincidence of interests to serve Cambodia's purpose. The only optimistic factor was the apparent willingness of the Chinese Government to accede to the participation of the Saigon regime in a Geneva-type conference.[16] Sihanouk's problem was to get agreement to the conference before such willingness changed to opposition, for if the Chinese were not prepared to permit representation of South Viet-Nam, there would be no hope whatsoever of American attendance. The United States, furthermore, was still opposed to a conference on Cambodia because it felt that such an occasion would be used by Communist representatives to exploit proposals for the neutralization of South Viet-Nam. In September, at a conference at Oxford University, U.S. Assistant Secretary of State for Far Eastern Affairs William P. Bundy had made his Government's position clear:

> As to Cambodia, our position is that the neutrality as well as the independence of Cambodia is prescribed in the 1954 accords. We ourselves issued a statement at that time indicating we would do nothing to upset these arrangements. We have in fact gone further and indicated our strong affirmative support for them, not once but many times. It does not therefore seem to us necessary that anything in the nature of a conference should be convened for that purpose.[17]

Sihanouk continued to demonstrate his disapproval of American policy. He attacked the United States for its involvement in South Vietnamese raids on Cambodian border villages. The raids were carried out with American "skyraiders," and Sihanouk alleged that they could not have taken place without the agreement of U.S. military headquarters in Saigon. Late in October, Sihanouk threatened to strike back "blow for blow" at any further aggression against Cambodia from South Viet-Nam by either American or South Vietnamese forces. As if to demonstrate that determination, Cambodian artillery shot down an American C-123 that strayed from South Vietnamese air space. Sihanouk repeated his threat to sever diplomatic relations with the United States and to recognize North Viet-Nam and the National Liberation Front and went out of his way to demand that the Geneva Conference on Indochina be reconvened to consider his charges against the United States and its involvement in border incidents.

In November, 1964, Sihanouk announced that he was inviting delegations from North and South Viet-Nam and Laos to attend an Indochinese People's Conference in Phnom Penh. He hoped that the meeting, which had probably been arranged during the discussions held in Peking,[18] would provide an opportunity for the National Liberation Front to confer with other dissident South Vietnamese groups and that they would agree to neutralize South Viet-Nam. In a direct sense, he saw the conference as an attempt to reconcile South Viet-Nam to the National Liberation Front and arrange a meeting at Geneva at which Cambodia's security needs would receive formal endorsement. Sihanouk described the forthcoming event as "the best method of compelling the United States to accept a peaceful solution for our region." [19] He assumed that South Vietnamese resistance to the Viet-Cong was tied to its association with the United States, and he reasoned that if he could induce a divorce, Cambodia might become the beneficiary. The end of the conflict would remove the prospect of a spreading conflagration and facilitate the recognition of frontiers and the continuing division of Viet-Nam as part of a general settlement. The fact that Sihanouk envisaged a South Vietnamese request that the Americans withdraw from that country was indicated by reports that the "Party for Peace" in Saigon, which included government members, might attend. A correspondent commented, "For the first time in the frustrating guerrilla war the Vietnamese on both sides would engage directly in open talks and possibly bring appreciably nearer the day when as some Americans fear, the Saigon Government itself will request them to go home." [20] The United States had been opposing a Geneva conference on Cambodia because of its probable effect on the determination of the Saigon regime. The organizers of the Phnom Penh conference reasoned that if the Saigon regime itself decided on neutralization, the United States would have little alternative but to accept its wishes. It is also possible, of course, to explain the announcement of the Indochinese People's Conference as simply another means of pressuring the United States to accept a Geneva conference.

The United States responded to the call for a conference by suggesting talks to relax the tension between Cambodia and the United States. Sihanouk agreed to this proposal, and discussions were scheduled to be held in New Delhi. The United States was anxious, according to Sihanouk, to keep open lines of communication with Cambodia. Certainly the Americans wished to avoid a total break, if only to forestall a situation in which Cambodia would openly become a sanctuary for the National Liberation Front. Sihanouk pressured the United States before the meeting in New Delhi by threatening to recognize both North Viet-Nam and the National Liberation Front if he failed to obtain satisfaction at the meeting. To make his point, at the end of November he sent his Foreign Minister, Huot Sambath, to Peking to begin discussions with representatives of the Hanoi Government and the National Liberation Front. The announced border agreements did not materialize, however, and when delegates from the United States and Cambodia met in New Delhi in mid-December, Sihanouk had not come to an agreement with the Communist Vietnamese.

The New Delhi meeting proved to be a fruitless exercise. Although the atmosphere was cordial, it was impossible to establish a basis of agreement from which the two countries could begin to normalize their relations. The discussions broke down over the question of border incidents with South Viet-Nam and the alleged use of Cambodian territory by the Viet-Cong; the United States was unwilling to accept responsibility for South Vietnamese actions in pursuit of Viet-Cong insurgents. It was only a matter of days before the now normal pattern of relations was re-established.

At the end of December, Cambodia complained of another incident along the border with South Viet-Nam, and Sihanouk threatened to break off diplomatic contact with the United States if one more Cambodian was killed in such an attack. In a speech opening the eighteenth National Congress, he said that his country was the object of a new campaign of hostilities "by South Viet-Nam, Thailand, the Secretary-General of SEATO, and the Khmer Serai, of which the strings are no doubt still being pulled by the United States." [21] Meanwhile, the Cambodian Government continued to make conciliatory gestures to China and its allies. It welcomed the Chinese "bomb of peace" and exchanged ambassadors with North Korea. The National Congress passed a unanimous motion condemning the sentencing of nine Chinese nationals by a Brazilian military court on charges of espionage. At the same time, Sihanouk renewed a characteristic practice of sending stinging and almost hysterical letters to the American press [22] in response to the recurrent charge that Viet-Cong were being supplied with weapons through Cambodia.

Much of Sihanouk's activity had been devoted to putting off the inevitable. Although he envisaged the prospect of a National Liberation Front victory, he also thought it possible to retain the division of Viet-Nam and to place a neutralized southern portion between Cambodia and North Viet-Nam. He had advanced this position since the end of 1963, when President de Gaulle first suggested neutralization as a solution to the problem of Indochina. [23]

The Indochina People's Conference demonstrated the growing conflict of interest between Cambodia and the Vietnamese Communists. Sihanouk conceived of the conference as a means to give expression to local Indochinese sentiment for neutralization and especially for neutralization of South Viet-Nam. To this end, he invited a number of dubious minority groupings to which even the Communist representatives took exception. Also represented at the conference were the Pathet Lao, the North Vietnamese Father-land Front, and the National Liberation Front for South Viet-Nam. Cambodia was represented by members of Sangkum. The Saigon Government had no representation, but there were three non-Communist delegations of South Vietnamese, two of which were composed of exiles living in Paris.

Sihanouk sought to channel the energies of the conference in the direction of his proposals for neutralization. He prepared a speech advocating the neutralization of the whole of Indochina, with the significant exception of North Viet-Nam, to be guaran-teed by both East and West, but he was never to deliver this piece of special pleading. On the eve of the conference, representatives of the National Liberation Front advanced strong objections to the text of the speech. Supported in their position by a message to the conference from Chou En-lai, they threatened to walk out of the chamber if Sihanouk delivered his address. Discussion of this issue delayed the opening session of the conference four days, but in the end the National Liberation Front, strongly supported by the North Vietnamese delegation, had its way. As a result, when the conference finally began its deliberations in early March, Si-hanouk had to be content to circulate and not deliver his speech.[24]

The proceedings of the conference demonstrated that both the North Vietnamese and the National Liberation Front were closely united in their opposition to negotiated settlement in Viet-Nam, which they had once advocated. The American bombing of North Viet-Nam had begun in February, and it is reasonable to assume that this change in the character of the war in Viet-Nam had re-sulted in a hardening of the terms of settlement by the Vietnamese Communists. Now both the Fatherland Front and the National Liberation Front, backed by China, called for the immediate, un-conditional, and total withdrawal of American forces from South Viet-Nam. This demand was, of course, directly opposed to Siha-nouk's suggestions that there should be a military disengagement by both sides in South Viet-Nam as a preliminary to a settlement there. Sihanouk reportedly said that he was fully aware that if the United States left South Viet-Nam, "we shall be face to face with Communism and with Vietnamese Communism. . . . That," he added, "is the most terrible kind."[25] He had set his sights high and had been disappointed. His only consolation was the conference's final resolution calling for a new Geneva conference "to afford the Kingdom of Cambodia legitimate guarantees concerning her neutrality and territorial integrity." [26] With this document—endorsed by the Communist representatives—he set out again to persuade the major powers that it was necessary to hold a conference on Cambodia. This time roles were reversed, and the Communists proved to be more obstructionist than the Americans.

Diplomatic Deadlock

One of the more significant legacies of the 1954 Geneva Conference was the establishment of the institution of co-chairmen. Britain and the Soviet Union, as the more moderate members of the opposing camps, assumed the positions, and their cooperation enabled the procedural machinery of the conference to function smoothly. The co-chairmen subsequently assumed other duties, particularly the joint responsibility for calling additional international meetings.[27]

For some time both the British and Soviet governments had been convinced that a conference on Cambodia would be useful. In the past, the Soviet Union had been more openly enthusiastic than Britain in seeking to promote this meeting. Britain, while agreeing in principle to a conference, had been inhibited from participating in a joint request for its convening because of the firm objections of the United States. On April 25, 1965, however, the British Government announced that it had accepted a Soviet draft text of a proposed joint message to members of the 1954 Geneva Conference and that it had asked the Soviet Government to agree to its immediate issue by the two co-chairmen. The British change of front [28] was admittedly the outcome of the condition of the war in Viet-Nam and the concurrent desire of the United States Government to seek a political solution. America's allies Thailand and South Viet-Nam were persuaded of the desirability of negotiation from a position of strength. On April 7, President Johnson had offered "unconditional discussions" [29] and was clearly looking for a way out of a war that seemed never-ending. In April, the British Government had sent former Foreign Secretary Patrick Gordon Walker on a tour of Southeast Asia in the hope of finding some means of beginning discussions on Viet-Nam. The tour was less than fruitful, because the governments in Hanoi and Peking refused him entry. Before leaving London, however, Gordon Walker had suggested that if it proved impossible to obtain a direct approach to the question of Viet-Nam, a conference on another Indochinese country (Laos was mentioned as a possibility) might provide a point of entry for discussions on Viet-Nam. Because of the final resolution of the Indochinese Poeple's Conference and the favorable Communist response, the British Government quickly realized that circumstances were far more propitious for beginning conversations on Viet-Nam as the outcome of a conference on Cambodia. When British Prime Minister Harold Wilson was in Washington in mid-April, he secured the agreement of President Johnson to this "oblique approach," [30] expecting that the terms for talks on Viet-Nam might emerge in the process.

The British response to the Soviet initiative did not in fact result in joint action on the draft message. The Soviet draft had appeared on April 3; the British reply came three weeks later. During the intervening period, a significant change in diplomatic positions took place. The net effect was to make the Soviet Government diffident about proceeding with the course of action it had suggested at the beginning of April. In the past, the British Government had been somewhat equivocal in its attitude toward a conference on Cambodia because of American objections. Now the situation was reversed, and the Soviet Union found its freedom of diplomatic movement restricted because of North Vietnamese and Chinese objections.

The Soviet draft message of April 3 was in response to a request from the Cambodian Foreign Minister to the co-chairman to re-convene the Geneva Conference in accordance with the general resolution of the Indochinese People's Conference. At the same time, the Foreign Minister had written to his Chinese counterpart seeking support for a Geneva meeting. The Chinese reply approved the idea of a conference and agreed that nine powers should be represented at it, rather than the fourteen who made up the conference on Laos.[31] The response also seemed to indicate that the participants in the proposed conference on Cambodia should be the nine countries that had taken part in the 1954 Geneva Conference on Indochina. This would have included the Government of South Viet-Nam. The Soviet draft of April 3 was more specific on the question of composition, referring to "the Governments of the countries that took part in the Geneva Conference of 1954." [32] By implication, this excluded the National Liberation Front.

At the Indochinese People's Conference, the position of the North Vietnamese and National Liberation Front representatives was that negotiations on Viet-Nam had to be preceded by withdrawal of American forces. But with the prospect of a conference on Cambodia turning into an informal conference on Viet-Nam, it became necessary to reiterate this position in advance of its meeting. The North Vietnamese did not want to witness a recurrence of the 1954 situation, when great power interests forced them to make substantial concessions. On this occasion, however, they were more fortunate, because the Chinese Government was determined to help them achieve their aims.

The views of the Chinese, the North Vietnamese, and the National Liberation Front on the question of a conference on Cambodia were made known to Sihanouk in the middle of April while he was in Djakarta to celebrate the tenth anniversary of the Bandung Conference. Sihanouk, who was embarrassed by press speculation that the conference on Cambodia was to be no more than a pretext for negotiations on Viet-Nam, heeded Communist objections, and on his return to Phnom Penh announced that he did not wish a conference on Cambodia to be the bait for a discussion on Viet-Nam. He then stated that if there was to be a conference on Cambodia, neither the United States nor South Viet-Nam should attend.

The question of the composition of the proposed conference eventually was responsible for its miscarriage. The active backers of the insurgents in the Viet-Nam conflict—determined to obstruct negotiations unless they were conducted on their own terms—felt it was necessary to prevent a conference on Cambodia. The Cambodian Government, for its part, had become so dependent on Communist good will and was so hopeful of regularizing its relations with the future masters of Viet-Nam that it had to accede on a matter to which the Communists appeared to attach so much importance.

When Gordon Walker visited Phnom Penh on April 26, Sihanouk refused to see him. He met only with the Foreign Minister, who expressed his concern about the desirability of a conference in view of undue press speculation about the nature of the meeting. The British emissary was prepared for this reservation and presented an *aide mémoire* which, besides indicating British acquiescence to the long-standing Cambodian request for a conference, stated: "Her Majesty's Government do not intend to propose the inclusion in the agenda of any questions not directly related to the independence, neutrality and territorial integrity of Cambodia." [33] The British attempt to reassure the Cambodians was of no avail. On May 1, the Cambodian Government altered its original position on the conference, now insisting on three prerequisites to a conference:

(1) The conference envisaged must be on the model of that of Geneva on Indochina in 1954 and not that of Geneva of 1961-62.

(2) Cambodia will not accept the presence of the alleged Government of Saigon at the said conference.

(3) Cambodia refuses all overlapping of the questions of Viet-Nam and Laos into the discussions of her own problems. [34]

Conditions (1) and (3) were unexceptionable. One can sympathize with Sihanouk's irritation that the proposed conference on Cambodia was to be used to settle the Viet-Nam question,[35] although he was realistic enough to appreciate that a settlement in Viet-Nam was a vital precondition to an effective solution to Cambodia's security problems. The second condition was a clear indication that Cambodia would not agree to a conference except on Communist terms. For the United States to disavow the Saigon Government would be to abdicate its position in Viet-Nam and to undermine whatever little legitimacy the prevailing military junta enjoyed. The Cambodian condition was acutely embarrassing to the Soviet Union, which, in its initial approach to the British Government on April 3, had implied that South Viet-Nam, as a participant in the 1954 Geneva Conference, would also be eligible to attend the proposed conference on Cambodia.

The enunciation of Cambodia's conditions for a conference was followed the next day by a supporting statement from the Chinese Government. The Chinese statement described American support for a conference on Cambodia as an attempt "to open up a way for its fraud of peace talks on the Viet-Nam question." The statement made it clear that China would be a party to discussions on Cambodia only if the United States was prepared to abdicate its position in Viet-Nam. It also presented another condition, which was implicit in the second Cambodian condition: "South Viet-Nam must be represented by the South Viet-Nam National Front for Liberation." [36] The same stipulation on representation was made in a note sent to the Cambodian Foreign Minister by the Hanoi Government. By that time, it was abundantly clear that a conference on Cambodia was out of the question. The Cambodian problem was now inextricably linked with the question of Viet-Nam, and on the matter of representation from South Viet-Nam neither side in the conflict was prepared to abandon its nominee. The Cambodians, caught in the middle of this diplomatic battle, had no alternative but to take a position that would be regarded with sympathy in Peking. As if to assure Communist China of its consistent posture, Cambodia severed diplomatic relations with the United States on May 3. After years of threats and warnings, Sihanouk had at last taken a step that seemed to many to tie him irretrievably to Peking.

The actual cause of the break was the publication of an article in *Newsweek* that allegedly contained insulting remarks about the Queen Mother. There was also another bombing incident along the border with South Viet-Nam. Sihanouk considered these two episodes sufficient provocation to justify the diplomatic rupture. The timing of the break, however, would seem to suggest that Sihanouk thought it politic to make another gesture of good will in the direction of Peking. He did not, however, accept the full embrace of Peking. He sought to continue consular relations with the United States, but Washington was not prepared to accept what was convenient for Sihanouk and a humiliation for itself. In refusing this request, U.S. Secretary of State Dean Rusk pointed out that normal relations with Cambodia were not possible unless they were mutual and reciprocal.

Meanwhile, the British Government attempted to salvage the conference. Prime Minister Harold Wilson wrote to Sihanouk on May 11 that there had been no communication from the Cambodian foreign ministry since the message to the co-chairman on March 15. Sihanouk's reply a few days later made it clear that Cambodia would not proceed with a conference against China's wishes. He pointed out, with some justice, that since the initial demand for a conference in 1962, "important changes have taken place in our region." He continued: "The Socialist Powers in particular have hardened their attitude toward American aggression against the D.R.V. and the progress of the N.L.F. in South Viet-Nam and have clearly stated their intention no longer to accept the Saigon Government as a participant in any conference on Cambodia. Cambodia herself has been obliged to note that this Government no longer controls the greater part of the Vietnamese frontier with Cambodia." This last sentence was most revealing, considering the constant Cambodian charge that the South Vietnamese Government was seeking to expand westward at Cambodia's expense and that the frontier incidents were evidence of this intention. Sihanouk obviously saw the Vietnamese *bête noir* operating from Hanoi rather than from ineffectual Saigon. He presented a list of alternatives that might solve the problem of representation at a conference on Cambodia, but it became obvious that the initiative was not his and that he was a prisoner of circumstances. He expressed his willingness to accept any solution on representation of South Viet-Nam that would be adopted "by agreement between the Great Powers of the East and West." [37] This was an admission that there was no immediate future for a conference to secure his country's neutrality.

The British Government received an equally unsatisfactory response when it sought to elicit an indication of the Soviet position. Diplomatic exchanges continued through May and June, but the Soviet Government showed no willingness to dispatch the joint message convening the conference. Despite British insistence that a conference devoted only to the question of Cambodia would improve the political atmosphere in Indochina, the Soviet Union was not willing to move. British support of American bombing in North Viet-Nam discouraged the Russians from associating now with the joint venture. Chinese and North Vietnamese opposition except on their terms for South Vietnamese representation had placed the Soviet Government in an impossible position, unless it wished to justify Chinese charges that it was a lackey of American imperialism.

For Sihanouk, this outcome of so much diplomatic effort was an unhappy state of affairs. As he stated in a letter to *The New York Times*, "The National Liberation Front and the Socialist Camp, confident in their imminent victory, are no longer interested, for their part, in a compromise solution." This meant that the question of Cambodia's security could not be settled independent of the conflict in Viet-Nam. Here the positions of the contending parties were so diametrically opposed that only a dramatic change in the military situation could bring the contestants to the conference table. For Cambodia, an agreement on neutrality required the agreement of the Great Powers, but because of their involvement in Viet-Nam, this was impossible. In the circumstances, Sihanouk had no alternative but to bow to what he regarded as inevitable Communist success and to rely for his country's future on continuing good relations with Communist countries, in particular with the Chinese People's Republic.

9

How to Stay Neutral

Cambodian foreign policy may be described as a process of sensitive response to those aspects of political change that bear on the security of the Khmer state. The most significant response of this kind was the recognition and acceptance of Chinese suzerainty in Southeast Asia at a time when Communist insurgent forces in neighboring countries seemed on the brink of military and political success. Cambodia's relationship with China was an attempt to mitigate the effect of political change, particularly the form Sihanouk expected it to take in Viet-Nam. Sihanouk viewed China as the only power capable of restraining the traditional expansion of the Vietnamese. He confided to a German visitor: "When the Americans leave without guarantees of non-Communism and territorial integrity to South Viet-Nam, Cambodia will be face to face with Communism along her entire Eastern border. This will be very dangerous for Cambodia, which does not want to become Communist. And for us in Cambodia, of all possible Communism, Viet-Nam [*sic*] Communism is the worst." [1]

By the end of 1965, despite American bombing of North Viet-Nam and reinforcement of American ground troops in South Viet-Nam, Sihanouk was still convinced, at least in public, that Cambodia would face Communism along its Eastern border. He told

172

a correspondent: "The Americans can murder ten or twenty million Vietnamese. But sooner or later, they will be forced to abandon Viet-Nam to the survivors. . . . The United States have launched themselves into an adventure which will inevitably end in defeat." [2]

In Sihanouk's eyes, China was the only country capable of restraining the Vietnamese from re-establishing a traditional pattern of westward movement. For the time being, it served China's purpose to preserve an independent, non-Communist Cambodia. Within the Afro-Asian world, there were very few non-Communist countries willing to act as spokesmen for the Chinese point of view. In this role, Cambodia performed a function that China wished to sustain. The Cambodians were happy to adopt the role of spokesman for China; it brought security and also valuable time.

After the failure to convene a conference on Cambodia, Sihanouk continued to demonstrate his country's value to Peking. In May, 1965, at the opening of the National Assembly, he announced proposals that Cambodia intended to sponsor at the Afro-Asian conference that was scheduled to be held in Algiers. He suggested that all countries claiming to be anti-imperialist should:

(1) quit the headquarters of the United Nations in New York and insist that the organization's offices be transferred to Geneva;

(2) reject American aid in all and any form; and

(3) sever, so far as possible, all relations with the United States, "in order to hasten the defeat of the imperialists." [3]

In June, Cambodia sent a delegation to an international conference for solidarity with the people of Viet-Nam in Hanoi and also dispatched a gift of pharmaceuticals for "innocent victims of the United States criminal air raids." [4] In that month, Cambodia's representative at the United Nations voted against an Indian resolution in the disarmament commission deploring nuclear tests that had taken place despite General Assembly motions. In September, Cambodia again sponsored Communist China's entry into the United Nations. After the negative vote on this issue, the Cambodian representative announced that his country would boycott all working committees of the General Assembly on the ground that the organization was "ineffective." [5] On the other hand, he made it plain that Cambodia did not intend to leave the United Nations, but would continue to participate in plenary meetings.

Sihanouk had no intention of becoming a Chinese puppet, but he was willing to make gestures that brought more gain than loss. He was anxious to provide for his country's security and even willing to speculate about Cambodia's becoming the Albania of Southeast Asia, but he sought to avoid the necessity of becoming a satellite in practice. As he told U.S. Senator Mike Mansfield, "Cambodia is too deeply attached to its independence to feel affection for countries that seek to reduce us to the position of a satellite." [6] Cambodia's gestures in China's interest did not commit it unconditionally. Indeed, it appears that the Chinese were as anxious as the Cambodians that the Khmer state should not appear to be acting as a duplicate of North Viet-Nam. According to one source, "Premier Chou En-lai privately has told Prince Sihanouk that their partnership would be served best if Cambodia retained her professed status as a neutral nation." [7]

After late 1965, Cambodia's association with China as a non-Communist country became increasingly valuable. Both North Korea and North Viet-Nam had become more responsive to Soviet overtures as China had demonstrated its inability to do more than offer good advice to its southern neighbor under fire from American bombs. On October 1, the abortive coup in Indonesia was crushed by the army, and that country not only withdrew from the Peking-Djakarta Axis, but also began a virulent internal campaign against local Communists and Chinese. In the coming months, China suffered serious diplomatic setbacks in Africa and experienced the humiliation of seeing a procession of its representatives dispatched back to Peking. In February, 1966, a similar experience befell China in Cuba.

Cambodia needed China, and at that point China regarded Cambodia as a valuable ally. The Chinese recognized this situa-

tion in October, 1965, when they invited Sihanouk to preside as
guest of honor at celebrations marking the sixteenth anniversary
of China's national day. Sihanouk was accorded excessive deference. He was met on arrival by Chairman Liu Shao-chi and Premier Chou En-lai, both of whom spent many days with their Cambodian guest. Sihanouk reciprocated by continuing to make the
right gestures. He backed China's successful demand for the postponement of the Afro-Asian conference. He lent his name to a
joint statement implying that the Soviet Government was soft on
imperialism and had been lacking in support for North Viet-Nam.[8]
This venture brought a direct snub from the Soviet Government,
which unceremoniously canceled a visit to Moscow Sihanouk had
scheduled for the next month. The excuse that the Soviet leaders
were very busy and so unable to meet him as planned was a clear
affront to Sihanouk's dignity. Indeed, so much was he annoyed
that he canceled a tour of East European capitals scheduled to
follow the visit to Moscow. The Chinese were no doubt delighted
at this outcome.

It is very likely that Sihanouk came to recognize that he was
going too far in one direction. He could not have failed to notice
that Chinese benefactions of material assistance did not match
their protests and encouragement to the regime in Hanoi. At the
same time, the Chinese were powerless to assist their persecuted
overseas community in Indonesia. The Soviet snub may have confirmed a feeling that Cambodia was perhaps overcompromising
its freedom in terms of the benefits of the Chinese connection. It
is interesting to note that while Sihanouk was in Peking, the Cambodian News Agency published an article by him stating plainly
that his country had no intention of becoming a satellite of Communist China.

Sihanouk may perhaps be regarded as a barometer of political
change in Southeast Asia. He has a sensitive faculty that has so
far enabled him to adapt the policy of his country to every shift in
the balance of power. A number of factors may have suggested
that he could become less dependent on China, though any shift

in emphasis on his part was marginal. First of all, he now recognized that Cambodia was serving a useful function for the Chinese at a time when China was increasingly isolated in the Afro-Asian world. Indeed, Mao Tse-tung told Sihanouk in October, 1965, "Your visit represents a form of aid that you bring us." [9] Secondly, China had shown some weakness in the face of American action in Viet-Nam, and this may have caused Sihanouk to doubt China's ability to come to Cambodia's assistance should it ever prove necessary. Finally, there was now less certainty of an early Viet-Cong victory in South Viet-Nam. While the United States and the South Vietnamese were far from winning the war, so were the insurgents, who earlier in 1965 had been confident of victory. The United States had made little impact on civil government in the south, but the immediate outcome of the war was no longer a foregone conclusion. Sihanouk, whose first priority was the security of his kingdom, demonstrated an increasing flexibility with a sensitive grasp, as always, of geopolitical realities. He declared in his Independence Day speech in November, 1965, that it was possible to decry the Russians: "Why do we dare to do so? Because the Russians are far from us. Moreover, since they are not on good terms with China, they cannot cross China to come and hit us. In fact, we can display insolence toward the countries that are far from us. If we do so toward the countries that are near us, we will certainly encounter difficulties." [10] Nevertheless, in the same speech, he criticized Cambodia's Communists, describing them as the valets of North Viet-Nam.

In one way Sihanouk had found his freedom of action limited by China, and that was over the question of the conference to provide his country with a guarantee. The Chinese and the North Vietnamese had vetoed such a conference because of a dispute over representation from South Viet-Nam. Prince Sihanouk accepted their stand and wrote to Ho Chi Minh that the National Liberation Front was "the only authentic representative of the South Vietnamese people." [11] But such support brought him no nearer his goal. He wanted more than vague promises, but this the

Chinese and Vietnamese Communists were not prepared to offer. Sihanouk recognized that, because of the Communist involvement in Viet-Nam, he could not expect to influence their position. As long as a conference on Cambodia involved adjoining countries—specifically Viet-Nam—and as long as the Viet-Nam issue remained unresolved, China and North Viet-Nam could not be expected to abandon the National Liberation Front. If the position of the Viet-Cong became more difficult, this would even be an additional reason for supporters to insist on its recognition as the sole representative of the South Vietnamese people. The future looked bleak for Sihanouk, as there seemed no way either to deal with Cambodia in isolation from the Viet-Nam issue or to insulate the kingdom from the war raging to the east. The problem was not only that the security of Cambodia could not be assured until a settlement was reached in Viet-Nam, but that the scale of that war might change and involve Cambodia. Such was the alarming prospect in December, 1965, when a State Department spokesman announced that the U.S. Government respected Cambodia's territorial integrity, "but it left open the possibility that American forces in South Viet-Nam might fire across the Cambodian border in self-defense." [12] The possibility materialized in the following year.

Mending Fences

The visit to London in November, 1965, of Sonn Sann, the Vice-President of the Cambodian Council of Ministers, indicated that the Cambodian Government was eager to re-establish closer relations with the Western powers. Cambodia had withdrawn its ambassador and diplomatic mission from London at the end of 1963, but did not formally sever diplomatic relations. Sonn Sann's visit coincided with the presentation of a new ambassador, Sonn Voeunsai, who was also ambassador to France and who resided in Paris. The fact that Britain permitted such an arrangement indicated its desire to conciliate Cambodia. Nothing of political substance came of Sonn Sann's discussions with British Foreign Secretary Michael Stewart, but the meeting itself demonstrated the basic flexibility of Cambodian foreign policy, which did not equate neutrality with diplomatic isolation. Later in the year, Cambodia demonstrated that a diplomatic *rapprochement* with Britain did not prevent indulging in international gestures that, although inconsequential, drew applause from Afro-Asian and Communist nations. When Harold Wilson visited New York to speak on Rhodesia before the United Nations General Assembly in December, the Cambodian delegation participated in a walk-out initiated by African states as the British Prime Minister made his way to the podium. At the beginning of November, Cambodia had criticized Britain's attempt to turn the proposed conference on Cambodia into one on Viet-Nam. Yet despite what may have been regarded as irritating gestures, the priorities of the Cambodian Government had not altered, and in June, 1966, Britain announced that it would replace its chargé d'affaires in Phnom Penh with an ambassador.

Cambodia's reservation about a conference that also discussed Viet-Nam was a pose necessitated by the exigencies of the situation. Minister of Information Chea San commented more openly: "But nevertheless, Cambodia for its part, does not reject the eventual holding of such a conference, provided it is not solely a pretext for a discussion on Viet-Nam." [13] This statement seemed to indicate that the Cambodian Government would not be averse to discussions on Viet-Nam arising out of a conference on Cambodia, and that any objections to the form of a proposed international gathering were not of Cambodia's own making. Also, because of the deterioration of relations with the Soviet Union, one of the co-chairmen of the Geneva Conference, it was necessary to re-establish more friendly contact with Britain, the other co-chairman. Cambodia was beginning to feel the chill winds of isolation, and recognized the dangers of becoming alienated from both powers that had the responsibility for convening an international conference on any part of Indochina.

Cambodia and the War in Viet-Nam

Cambodia had sought to mend its fences with Britain, but such *rapprochement* had not borne fruit. For the time being, a conference was out of the question, and Cambodia was perched precariously on the sidelines of a war that periodically threatened to envelop it. On October 22, 1965, the International Control Commission in Cambodia reported to the co-chairmen on its investigations of incidents along the border of South Viet-Nam and Cambodia. It stated that Cambodia had reported 206 such incidents in 1963, 275 in 1964, and 385 up to May 31, 1965 (the date the report ended). Regarding eight major incidents between May, 1964, and May, 1965, the Commission "found conclusive evidence in these incidents that the armed forces of the Republic of South Viet-Nam were responsible for these violations. The Commission is also convinced that none of these incidents was provoked by the Royal Government of Cambodia." [14]

These border clashes arose from the South Vietnamese conviction that Cambodian territory was being used by the Viet-Cong, either as a sanctuary or as a means of communication, through which reinforcements could be introduced into South Viet-Nam from North Viet-Nam. The Cambodian Government has periodically invited correspondents of leading American newspapers to test for themselves the validity of such charges. While they cannot establish or deny the truth about the presence of mobile Viet-Cong bands that are believed to retreat, when pressed, into the difficult terrain of the border provinces, they have been able to check map references quoted by South Vietnamese and American sources indicating major bases. *The New York Times* correspondent Seymour Topping reported in October, 1965:

> . . . there are some remote jungle areas of the Cambodian-Viet-Nam border that are impossible to check for Viet-Cong activity and it is doubtful that even the Phnom Penh Government knows what transpires there. . . . Viet-Cong guerrillas are known to slip occa-

sionally into Cambodian frontier areas to evade pursuit or to out-
flank some Vietnamese position. It would be impossible for an army
20 times the size of the Cambodian force of 30,000 men to close the
border to such forays.[15]

While Topping was prepared to admit this degree of infiltration,
he found no evidence to substantiate the charge that Cambodia
served as a base for major Viet-Cong activity. Indeed, he confi-
dently asserted: "It is the consensus of Western diplomats and
independent observers stationed in Cambodia that the country is
not a major sanctuary or a major route for the delivery of military
equipment and supplies to the Viet-Cong. This was also the prevailing view among American officials posted in Phnom Penh prior
to the severance of diplomatic relations." [16]

The following month, however, there was increasing evidence
that the Viet-Cong was using Cambodian territory in the manner
that Topping admitted. After a major clash in the Ia Drang Valley,
between Viet-Cong and troops of the United States First Cavalry,
it was suggested that the remnants of the defeated Viet-Cong force
had retreated over the Cambodian border.[17] At the end of November, U.S. Under-Secretary of State U. Alexis Johnson revealed that
part of Cambodian territory was being watched by United States
aircraft and that they were authorized to return fire if attacked.
This announcement coincided with renewed charges by the governments of Thailand and South Viet-Nam that North Vietnamese lines of infiltration passed through Cambodia. To the hypersensitive Cambodians, these were alarming developments. They
had no desire to see a reunited Communist Viet-Nam; nor were
they willing to become the victims of attempts by those opposing
the Communists to seal off their frontiers.

The Cambodian Government demonstrated its nervousness
time and time again in reaction to what it considered pointers to
action by its neighbors with possible American backing. At the end
of November, 1965, for example, Joseph Alsop claimed in the *New
York Herald Tribune* that Cambodia was supplying the Viet-Cong
with Chinese arms through the port of Sihanoukville. Cambodia

vehemently denied this charge and proposed to the president of
the International Control Commission that his organization ensure
strict control of landings at Sihanoukville and make public its
findings. In May, 1966, *New York Times* correspondent C. L. Sulzberger aroused Cambodian ire by claiming that a Viet-Cong supply
route called the "Sihanouk Road" passed from Laos through the
province of Stung Treng.[18]

Cambodian fears had been intensified following a State Department announcement that military commanders had the authority
to take action to protect their forces. This announcement was
interpreted in Cambodia as a green light to "violate our frontiers
and exercise on our territory the alleged right of hot pursuit under
the fallacious pretext of self-defense." [19] The United States Government, itself anxious to prevent Cambodia from becoming involved
in the Viet-Nam War, accordingly began to realize that its announcement of the right to pursue Viet-Cong units across the
Cambodian border had only aggravated the situation. Calmer
counsel prevailed, and the United States officially recognized that
Cambodia was not conniving with the Viet-Cong, but that it had
a difficult task in seeking to patrol a long inhospitable frontier
region. At the same time, it clarified its announced policy of hot
pursuit: A government spokesman said that American troops
would not trespass across the frontier, but "only return fire in tactical situations." [20]

The United States was eager to obtain a working arrangement
with Cambodia to seal off the Cambodian-Vietnamese frontier. If
effective, this would solve the problem of Viet-Cong retreat and
also avoid continued difficulties with the Cambodian Government.
Sihanouk had made a vague suggestion that a "peace force" stationed along the frontier with South Viet-Nam might be provided
from the resources of the International Control Commission. The
problem was similar to earlier difficulties blocking the agreement
to convene a conference on Cambodian neutrality. The co-chairmen, who supervised the activities of the Commission, would
have to support any new role the International Control Commis-

sion took on. The composition of the Commission was such that the North Vietnamese and the Chinese regarded it as a hostile rather than a neutral body. Its three members were Poland, India, and Canada. The prospect of India and Canada outvoting Poland, meant that the Soviet Union was not in a position to support plans for an observer force, even if this was a practical proposition. The position of the Cambodian Government was equally difficult because it could not afford openly to alienate the National Liberation Front for fear that it might extend its activities to Cambodia and also because its long-run prospects were still bright in South Viet-Nam. Cambodia could not become an active party to what might well be construed as precautionary measures against the Viet-Cong. The existing situation was dangerous, but it could be tolerated as long as the Americans recognized, at least publicly, that Cambodia was not implicated in Viet-Cong border crossings. While this was so, there was little point in initiating a frontier patrol under the control of the International Control Commission, action which might be interpreted as lending assistance to the enemies of the National Liberation Front. On January 26, 1966, the Cambodian Foreign Ministry announced that it could not agree to grant wider powers to the International Control Commission with the aim of turning it into a police force to protect the Cambodian frontier, thus exceeding the powers that had been assigned by the Geneva Agreements of 1954. This statement was reported favorably in the North Vietnamese press.[21]

Since the beginning of 1966, the British Government had been trying without success to persuade the Cambodians that it would be in their own interests to see an enlargement of the Commission. The Cambodians were not enthusiastic at this suggestion, for they still had some hope of securing written recognition of their frontiers from the Vietnamese Communists. In an attempt to expedite matters, the Cambodian Government in April elevated the status of the North Vietnamese commercial representative in Phnom Penh to that of diplomatic representative. This was a minor concession, as the recognition corresponded only to the status enjoyed by South Viet-Nam's representative before the diplomatic rupture in August, 1963. The gesture was nonetheless an indication of Cambodia's good intentions. In May, 1966, it was made public that a treaty of friendship and nonaggression was to be signed shortly between Cambodia, North Viet-Nam, and the National Liberation Front. The Communists did not immediately respond to this initiative, and in the following September, the eighth in a series of negotiations between Cambodian and National Liberation Front representatives was adjourned inconclusively.[22] It became increasingly clear that they had no desire to offer Sihanouk firm written assurances for the future. Sihanouk therefore played what the Cambodian press described as his last card in the attempt to maintain a disengaged kingdom.[23]

Sihanouk had been increasingly alarmed at charges that his kingdom was being used as a transit route and sanctuary for Viet-Cong and North Vietnamese regulars. He was concerned at the prospect of American intervention, particularly after he received a note from Washington protesting Viet-Cong use of Cambodian territory.[24] He was also worried by the possibility that American successes in the war in South Viet-Nam might force the Communists to try to make increasing use of Cambodian territory. In any event, the war would spread, and Cambodia would become a helpless victim of any escalation. By June, 1966, it appeared that Cambodian concern about the possible extension of the Viet-Nam war was beginning to take precedence over regard for Vietnamese Communist sensibilities. On June 25, the Cambodian Government made a formal request to the co-chairmen of the Geneva Conference to reinforce the International Control Commission along the Cambodian-Vietnamese border. The United States Government had already made known its willingness to defray the expenses of this reinforcement. Cambodia's object was to establish good faith with the United States and demonstrate its restraint from positive involvement in the Viet-Nam conflict. At the same time, enlargement of the Commission could make it more difficult for the Viet-Cong to use Cambodian territory to any substantial degree. Cambodia's initiative unfortunately remained suspended because the Soviet Union, as one of the co-chairmen, had no desire

to antagonize the North Vietnamese, who were adamantly opposed to what they regarded as a concession to the United States.
The Soviet Union was also disinclined to lay itself open again to
Chinese charges of abetting imperialism; consequently, it made
known its opposition to the proposal. The incident demonstrated
the disadvantage of neutrality when an action that will serve the
interests of a neutral state depends on the approval of antagonistic
powers, one of which feels its own interests will suffer by ac-
quiescing.

There is little the Cambodian Government can do of its own
accord to provide satisfactory safeguards for Cambodia's security;
it is very much a prisoner of unfortunate circumstances. To its
credit and to that of Norodom Sihanouk, Cambodia has remained
independent and stable while much of Indochina is in turmoil. It
has achieved this by seeking to avoid antagonizing those forces
that are most capable of threatening its independent position.
Minister of Information Chea San pointed out: "The secret of our
success is to be found in our firm and unfaltering grasp of realities
and in the fact that we never lose sight of the possibilities open to
our country, nor of the fluctuations taking place in the outside
world." [25] A policy of responding to the prevailing wind, however,
is likely to induce a certain rigidity in diplomatic positions, particularly if the assumption underlying the policy is that the prevailing
wind represents a permanent state of affairs. The establishment
and maintenance of a neutral position, as we have noted, depends
on the creation of an equilibrium by opposing political forces of
approximate strength. Cambodian foreign policy has moved beyond the equilibrium stage and seeks to secure Cambodia's future
by establishing ties with those who will interpose themselves
between the Khmer State and its neighbors who, in varying
ideological guises, would be easily disposed to stamp out Cambodia's national existence. Sihanouk is acutely conscious of the
fact that it was only the French protectorate that preserved Cambodia's independent identity from the territorial aggrandizement
of Siam and Annam. In the twentieth century, he sees China in

the role of France, and regards its more recent setbacks, including the convulsions of the cultural revolution, as only short-term phenomena. For this reason, Cambodia is forced to proceed on a dependent course. Sihanouk has stated: "If we accept American aid, even without conditions, the Communist powers will not look favorably at this 'return' and will harden their attitude to us and sponsor subversion, infiltration, and insecurity in Cambodia." [26]

Meanwhile, Sihanouk may derive certain comfort from historic trends. He sees the future in terms of relationships between national states and believes that Communism has failed to take root as a universal phenomenon. Cambodia's relations with governments, regardless of their political persuasions, in Thailand and Viet-Nam are not expected to be harmonious. On the other hand, if history is a guide, relations between China and a reunited Viet-Nam need not be harmonious.

Sihanouk wants to maintain the *status quo* as far as Cambodia is concerned, in the hope that he can profitably use the time he gains to develop the national economy and to produce the sense of well-being so vital to the preservation of genuine national unity. He hopes that Cambodia can survive intact and without becoming physically involved in the conflict that is progressing across its borders. When a political solution is found for the war in Viet-Nam, Cambodia will have to reassess its foreign policy in terms of the prevailing configuration of power. In the meantime, foreign policy must be a reactive process in the light of long-term trends and day-to-day contingencies, the most alarming of which is the war in Viet-Nam.

Cambodia's political future seems to be linked inextricably with the conflict being waged to the east. Any settlement satisfying Cambodia's minimum security requisites will have to wait until there is a resolution of the Viet-Nam question. The problem for Cambodia is to remain detached and intact until a more permanent arrangement for the peaceful and independent existence of the states of Indochina is decided by the powers concerned.

10

Conclusion

The principal objective of Cambodian foreign policy is not a mysterious secret; it is publicized. The Cambodian Government has clearly expressed, by word and deed, its desperate concern to protect and preserve a territorial integrity that has been subject to political erosion for centuries. Over one hundred years ago, this process of erosion was brought to a halt by the French imperial mission in Asia, which restrained traditional pressures and effected a measure of territorial reclamation. Today, free from the protective overlordship of the colonial power, Cambodia has to cope independently with the reappearance of traditional antagonisms, albeit in modern guise.

Cambodia sees itself threatened on the north and west by Thai irredentism, and on the east by Vietnamese expansionism, which Cambodians expect will again come into full play when Viet-Nam is reunited. Sihanouk is constantly seeking to remind his fellow countrymen of these dangers to Cambodia's national survival and to impress upon them that the danger is not moderated by ideological orientation. In June, 1966, he advised the graduates of the Cambodian Military Academy, "Whatever ideologies they may embrace, Thailand and Viet-Nam will always be themselves and by all means will try incessantly to wipe Cambodia from the face

186

and history of the world." [1] Sihanouk sees his country as engaged not in mere border conflicts or even bitter but conventional diplomatic exchanges, but in a virtual life-and-death struggle for the survival of Cambodia as a physical entity. Because of its deep concern that neighboring countries are actively committed to dismembering it, Cambodia, like the state of Israel, cannot take its future territorial integrity for granted. Cambodia's statesmen are constantly troubled by a nightmare of its two rapacious neighbors dividing the country between them along the line of the Mekong River.

Since Cambodia's neighbors and traditional enemies are aligned with one or another of the great powers, the initial purpose of Cambodia's neutrality was to effect a balance between the powers, as represented by the Communists and the United States. Implementation of the policy of neutrality proved, however, to be more than a simple matter of attempting to steer a middle course in the Cold War. Cambodia's master mariner was obliged to revise his policy as a result of the situation in Southeast Asia. Within a relatively short time after Cambodia achieved its independence, he was convinced that the forthcoming balance of power in the area would reflect the superior position of the Communists and, in particular, the suzerain role of the Chinese People's Republic. He came to regard the United States as incapable of effectively sustaining its allies in Indochina or of acting as a permanent counterpoise to Communist power. Hence, neutrality developed in protean form characterized less by conventional nonalignment than by a pattern of accommodation and deference to Communist diplomatic positions as long as these did not appear to imperil the existence of Cambodia. Indeed, Cambodia sought security against Communists from other Communists rather than from the United States.

For a number of years, the conduct of Cambodian foreign policy was predicated on the expectation that the National Liberation Front for South Viet-Nam would eventually triumph. Despite the continuing deployment of superior American fire-power both north and south of the Seventeenth Parallel, Sihanouk still retains that conviction. He has yet to be convinced that an American physical presence has the stoicism and tenacity to match that of the Vietnamese insurgents and so ensure the continued division of Viet-Nam. Ideally, he would prefer to see that division perpetuated,[2] for it would assuage Cambodian fears by providing a buffer between Cambodia and the Communist section of Viet-Nam, which is apparently more dynamic and cohesive than South Viet-Nam. Sihanouk has sought to promote such a state of affairs since 1960 by sponsoring proposals for a neutral zone to encompass South Viet-Nam, Laos, and Cambodia, but he has not yet received a uniform response from the principal antagonists in Southeast Asia. For the time being, North Viet-Nam, the National Liberation Front, and Communist China have all set themselves firmly against the convening of a conference through which Cambodia might receive satisfactory guarantees. Cambodia, for its part, has been obliged to defer to Communist priorities. Any grievance over the miscarriage of the conference proposal is directed, at least in public, against the government of the United States and not against the Communist states. Sihanouk has claimed many times that, had it not been for earlier American obstruction, his idea would have borne fruit. This is a debatable assumption. He may also be in error when he argues that the United States, by increasing the intensity and scale of conflict in Viet-Nam, has succeeded only in stimulating a tenacious and fanatical response that will eventually force the Americans to retire exhausted from the field of battle. For the time being he seems convinced of that outcome. His assessment is supported by the difficulties experienced in civil government in the urban areas of South Viet-Nam and by the continuing Viet-Cong control of a major portion of the countryside.

Cambodia's behavior has been colored by the prospect of having Vietnamese Communism along its eastern frontier. Cambodia has sought to come to terms with Hanoi before rather than after the expected departure of United States forces from South Viet-Nam. Sihanouk has sought formal written guarantees for Cambodia's present eastern frontiers (including its offshore islands) from North Viet-Nam and the National Liberation Front before they are in a position to dictate terms to Cambodia. So far, they have responded with verbal assurances only. Since the Vietnamese Communists also have not lost their conviction that the Americans will be the first to leave the field of battle,[3] they probably feel there is nothing of substance to be gained by an advance commitment to the present frontiers of Cambodia. Sihanouk, convinced that the N.L.F. is entrenched as his neighbor, cannot reject its verbal assurances and thereby risk incurring its animosity.[4]

Sihanouk has pledged his country's political support to the cause of the National Liberation Front and has backed this up with symbolic but minor gestures such as his message to Ho Chi Minh on the twelfth anniversary of the signing of the Geneva Agreements. Such a posture follows from Cambodia's need to avoid antagonizing the Vietnamese Communists. At the same time, Cambodia has had to face American, South Vietnamese, and Thai charges that it has actively cooperated with the Viet-Cong by placing its territory at their disposal. In order to moderate those charges, Sihanouk called for the enlargement of the International Control Commission to provide at least a political *cordon sanitaire* along the border with South Viet-Nam. To the National Liberation Front, such an initiative could be justified as an attempt to uphold the 1954 Geneva Agreements, which they claim to support. To the Americans and their allies, it demonstrated good faith concerning Viet-Cong use of Cambodian territory. In this way, Sihanouk has sought to avoid both a growing use of Cambodia by the Communist insurgents and the danger of an escalation of the Viet-Nam War into Cambodian territory. The maneuver has not succeeded, at least for the time being, because the Soviet co-chairman of the Geneva Conference would not consent to the proposal. Once again, Cambodia's search for security continued unrewarded.

Sihauouk's view of the future encompasses a Communist success in Viet-Nam and Chinese political dominance in Southeast Asia. His ultimate hopes for the future viability of Cambodia are founded on two premises: (1) that historic differences, rather than ideological affinity, will determine the relationship to be established between China and a reunited Viet-Nam; and (2) that China, conscious of the contagion of polycentrism and the subordination of Marxism-Leninism to national interests, will not wish to see a powerful Viet-Nam develop at the expense of the other Indochinese nations. Sihanouk expects that China, in its own interests, will seek to interpose its power and political presence between Cambodia and Viet-Nam. Only a direct quotation can convey the intensity with which this hope is expressed:

> La Chine, c'est en effet le synonyme de la survie du Cambodge (et pour l'instant même de la monarchie Khmer) dans l'indépendence, la paix, l'intégrité territoriale. Si nous éloignous de la Chine, nous sommes devôrés par les vauteurs que sont les eternels avaleurs de terre Khmère.[5]

For Cambodia, a close and harmonious association with China is absolutely vital, but such an association must be based on mutual convenience, not sentiment. Sihanouk has never deluded himself on this point. For Cambodia, the value of the association will depend on the unwillingness of China to sacrifice the smaller state's vital interests for some gain. As long as China is prepared and able to exercise restraint over the Vietnamese and, of course, the Thais, Cambodian policy toward China will be based on reciprocity. Indeed, such would appear to be the essence of policy toward a number of smaller states that have no direct national interest in Cambodia. Reciprocation toward China will continue to involve support for Chinese diplomatic positions, which is of some value coming from a non-Communist state. If China begins to treat Cambodia like a dispensable piece of real estate, mutual relations can be expected to alter. It is, however, questionable that, in such a case, Cambodia will be able to exercise any control over the situation. Without the ability to invoke countervailing power, Cambodia is dependent on Chinese good will.

One indication of Cambodia's apprehension over its future relationship with China concerns its northern and western frontiers.

Cambodia is genuinely afraid that China, which now sponsors the Thailand Patriotic Front, will seek increasingly to persuade the Thais of the virtues of a neutral or pro-Communist posture. Cambodia would like to see a genuinely neutral Thailand, free of American military bases and free of the pernicious and troublesome Khmer Serai. Yet it is alarmed by the prospect of a Thailand associated with China, a prospect more likely if ever the United States feels obliged to remove its military establishment from South Viet-Nam. The Thai Government would then, according to Sihanouk, adopt a so-called traditional policy of accommodation to the prevailing wind. In such circumstances, Thailand may be accorded a more benign regard by Peking than is Cambodia. Cambodians still fear that Thailand will eventually seek to retrieve those provinces the French restored to Cambodia in 1946. Cambodia is thus of two minds about Thailand. For cultural and political reasons, Sihanouk would like to establish a *modus vivendi* with the Thais, since Cambodians do not regard Thais with the same racial animosity as they do the Vietnamese. In June, 1966, Sihanouk held out the hand of friendship to Thailand, but Thailand rejected this offer on the grounds that Cambodia was too deeply involved with Communist countries. In time—that is, if there is time, and especially if the Thai monarchy plays a more prominent role in political life—a *rapprochement* may be possible. On the other hand, if Cambodian leaders were to choose between having Thailand as a neighbor aligned with China or with the United States, they would probably opt for the latter. In this way, Thailand's irredentist designs may be checked by continuing Chinese support for Cambodian territorial integrity against a mutual enemy.

For the time being, Cambodia remains perched in precarious fashion on the sidelines of a war that still threatens to engulf it, and the outcome of which may give Cambodians no satisfaction. It also has to face the periodic harassment of neighbors aligned with the West who distrust Cambodia for past and present associations. Through determined, if unconventional, leadership, it has been able to avoid the cauldron of conflict. Through a policy that combines long-term priorities and pragmatic, day-to-day decisions, it has preserved an independent existence—no mean achievement in the environment of Indochina. This existence is still tenuous, and the danger is far from removed that the modern Khmer State will suffer the same unfortunate fate as its illustrious forebear.

Notes

1. INTRODUCING CAMBODIA

1. For greater detail of village life, see May Ebihara, "Khmer," in Frank M. Lebar, Gerald C. Hickey, and John K. Musgrave, *Ethnic Groups of Mainland Southeast Asia* (New Haven: Yale University Press, 1964), pp. 92–105.

2. *Réalités cambodgiennes* (Phnom Penh), June 3, 1966.

3. C. Pym, *Mistapim in Cambodia* (London: Hodder and Stoughton, 1960), p. 179.

4. *Cambodia, Today and Yesterday* (Phnom Penh: Ministry of Information, n.d.), p. 3.

5. *The R.K.S.J. Today* (Phnom Penh), March, 1960.

6. *Kambuja* (Phnom Penh), December 15, 1966, p. 80.

7. Prince Norodom Sihanouk, "Cambodia Neutral: The Dictate of Necessity," *Foreign Affairs*, July, 1958, p. 583.

2. THE EMERGENCE OF INDEPENDENT CAMBODIA

1. For a fine history in English translation of the rise and fall of the Kambuja Empire, see George Coedès, *The Making of Southeast Asia*, trans. H. M. Wright (Berkeley, Calif.: University of California Press, 1966).

2. Note the account of the harsh system of taxation and the violent rural protest in 1925 in Kompong Chnang Province in Walter G. Langlois, *André Malraux: The Indochina Adventure* (New York: Frederick A. Praeger, 1966), pp. 188–99.

3. The Free French response to this event was the Brazzaville Declaration of March 24, which promised the establishment of an Indochinese Federation whose constituents would enjoy a large measure of autonomy, but as part of the new French Union. See "Declaration of the Provisional French Government Concerning Indochina; March 24, 1954," in Allan B. Cole (ed.), *Conflict in Indo-China and International Repercussions: A Documentary History, 1945–1955* (Ithaca, N.Y.: Cornell University Press, 1956), pp. 5–7. See also Ton That Thien, "The Influence of Indo-China on the Evolution of the French Union," *India Quarterly*, October–December, 1952.

4. For a short pen portrait, see Pierre Christian, "Son Ngoc Thanh," *Indochine sud est asiatique* (Saigon), October, 1952, pp. 48–49.

5. A prime concern of the British commander was to avoid civil disturbances at a time when Cambodia provided the main supply of fresh food to Saigon. See "Extract from the Report to the Combined Chiefs of Staff by the Supreme Allied Commander, Southeast Asia 30th June, 1947," in *Docu-*

ments Relating to British Involvement in the Indochina Conflict 1945–1965, Cmnd. 2834 (London: H.M.S.O., 1965) pp. 51–52.

6. See *L'Action de S.M. Norodom Sihanouk pour l'independence du Cambodge 1941–1955* (Phnom Penh: Cambodian Ministry of Information, 1959), p. 5.

7. *Ibid.*, p. 7.

8. Early in 1947, the King was reported to have said: "None is more desirous of complete independence than I, but we must look facts in the face. We are too poor to support or defend ourselves. We are dependent upon some major power to give us technicians and troops. If not France it would be some other great nation. We are a small power sandwiched between twenty million Annamese [sic] and twelve million Siamese." *The New York Times*, February 12, 1947.

9. *Neak Cheat Niyum (The Nationalist)* (Phnom Penh), August 25, 1963.

10. A valuable background to the emergence of the first political parties in Cambodia is in Philippe Preschez, *Essai sur la democratie au Cambodge* (Paris: Fondations Nationals des Sciences Politiques, 1961), pp. 16–18.

11. *L'Action de S. M. Norodom Sihanouk*, p. 11.

12. *Ibid.*, pp. 16–17.

13. Martin F. Herz, *A Short History of Cambodia* (New York: Frederick A. Praeger, 1958), p. 83, describes Son Ngoc Thanh's homecoming in terms of the arrival of a political messiah.

14. For an account of Communist-front activities in Cambodia, see Bernard B. Fall, *Le Viet-Minh* (Paris: Libraire Armand Colin, 1960), pp. 127–29.

15. See Norodom Sihanouk, *La Monarchie cambodgienne et la croisade royale pour l'indépendance* (Phnom Penh, n.d.), pp. 69–70.

16. April 19, 1953.

17. Sihanouk, *La Monarchie cambodgienne*, p. 85.

18. He pointed out, "We are not Communists but we do not have to take sides against Communism as long as the latter does not attempt to impose itself by force on our country." *Cambodian Neutrality* (London: Royal Embassy of Cambodia, n.d.), p. 7.

19. George Modelski (ed.), *SEATO: Six Studies* (Sydney: F. W. Cheshire, 1962), p. 142.

20. See U. S. Department of State, *American Foreign Policy, Current Documents, 1956* (Washington, D.C.: United States Government Printing Office, 1959), p. 790.

21. See Zolton M. Szaz, "Cambodia's Foreign Policy," *Far Eastern Survey*, October, 1955, p. 154.

22. See Jules Roy, *The Battle of Dienbienphu* (New York: Harper & Row, 1965), pp. 244–47.

23. Anthony Eden, *Memoirs: Full Circle* (New York: Houghton Mifflin, 1950), p. 106.

24. See Mathew B. Ridgway and H. H. Martin, *Soldier: The Memoirs of Mathew B. Ridgway* (New York: Harper & Row, 1956), pp. 275–76.

25. For an illuminating account of the negotiations on intervention, see Coral Bell, *Survey of International Affairs, 1954*, ed. F. C. Benham (London: Oxford University Press, 1957), pp. 21–42.

26. *The New York Times*, May 12, 1954.

27. *Documents Relating to the Discussion of Korea and Indo-China at the Geneva Conference*, April 27–June 15, 1954, Cmnd. 9186 (London: H.M.S.O.), p. 114. For a general account of the Geneva Conference, see Bell, *op. cit.*, pp. 42–73 and Donald Lancaster, *The Emancipation of French Indochina* (London: Oxford University Press, 1961), pp. 313–37.

28. Eden, *op. cit.*, p. 129.

29. *Ibid.*, p. 140.

30. *Further Documents Relating to the Discussion of Indochina at the Conference, June 16–July 21, 1954*, Cmnd. 9239 (London: H.M.S.O., 1954), p. 41.

31. Cambodia was the only one of the three Associated States to sign the Geneva Agreements in its own right as a sovereign power. In the case of Laos and (South) Viet-Nam, the agreements on the cessation of hostilities were signed by the Commander-in-Chief of the French Union forces.

3. CAMBODIA CHOOSES NEUTRALITY

1. Fall (*op. cit.*, p. 126) asserts that the Democratic Republic of Viet-Nam had combined its Marxist ideology with the traditional aims of Vietnamese nationalism. See also the documentary evidence in P. J. Honey, *Communism in North Viet-Nam* (Cambridge, Mass.: M.I.T. Press, 1963), pp. 25, 170; and George Modelski, "The Viet-Minh Complex," in Cyril E. Black and Thomas P. Thornton (eds.), *Communism and Revolution* (Princeton, N.J.: Princeton University Press, 1964). Modelski argues (p. 191) that the Viet-Minh "had ambitions to preserve the French created structure of the Indo-Chinese Federation under its own leadership."

2. "Since June [1954], the King has been vainly angling for an American commitment guaranteeing Cambodia's sovereignty and, in return, has indicated his country's willingness to join a Western security system for Southeast Asia." Virginia Thompson and Richard Adloff, *Minority Problems in South East Asia* (Stanford, Calif.: Stanford University Press, 1955), p. 196.

3. Szaz, *op. cit.*, pp. 153–54.

4. After Cambodia's success at Geneva, its ambassador in Washington officially conveyed his country's gratitude for American assistance and in turn received renewed assurances that the Southeast Asian Treaty Organization would guarantee Cambodia's independence. See *Modelski* (ed.), SEATO, p. 143.

5. *Department of State Bulletin XXXI*, No. 805 (November 29, 1954), p. 823.

6. Quoted in Denise Folliot, *Documents on International Affairs 1954* (London: 1957), p. 163.

7. *Loc. cit.*

8. A senior British service commander pointed out that the Manila Treaty "provides for the first time a United States commitment to assist in defending part of the mainland of Southeast Asia, and as a result has probably by its very existence eliminated, for the present at least, the danger of *open* aggression" (italics added). Royal Institute of International Affairs, Chatham House Study Group, *Collective Defense in South East Asia* (London: Oxford University Press, 1956), p. xiii.

9. The absence of supervision troubled the Cambodian Government, which

suspected that the Viet-Minh had merely merged with the Vietnamese minority. When it began to function, the Commission appeared satisfied with the progress of demobilization and withdrawal. See *First Progress Report of the International Commission for Supervision and Control in Cambodia for the Period ending December 31, 1954*, Cmnd. 9458 (London: H.M.S.O., 1955), pp. 5–6.

10. Szaz, *op. cit.*, p. 156.

11. *Second Progress Report of the International Commission for Supervision and Control in Cambodia for the Period January 1 to March 31, 1955*, Cmnd. 9534 (London: H.M.S.O., 1955), Appendix I, p. 39.

12. *The Hindustan Times* (New Delhi), April 3, 1956.

13. G. McT. Kahin, *The Asian-African Conference of April, 1955* (Ithaca, N.Y.: Cornell University Press, 1956), p. 13.

14. Sihanouk is alleged to have informed Laotian Prince Boun Oum that Chou had stated, "We do not mind the French, they are powerless to threaten China. But if you bring the Americans in we shall be obliged to attack you." Michael Field, *The Prevailing Wind* (London: Methuen, 1965), p. 201.

15. *Le Monde* (Paris), June 13, 1956.

16. *Third Interim Report of the International Commission for Supervision and Control in Cambodia for the period April 1 to July 28, 1955*, Cmnd. 9579 (London: H.M.S.O., 1955), pp. 5–9.

17. Editorial in *Jen-min Jih-pao* (*People's Daily*) (Peking), June 24, 1955. Quoted in *Survey of China Mainland Press*, No. 1077 (25/7, June, 1955), p. 39.

18. *The Hindu* (Madras), July 13, 1955.

19. Herz, *op. cit.*, p. 94.

20. The Commission reported, "Any informal suggestions that were made by the Commissioners in their individual capacity were meant to persuade the government before it took any final decisions to examine quietly and carefully the problem whether or not the royal reforms were compatible with the international obligations undertaken by Cambodia at the Geneva Conference." *Second Progress Report of the International Commission*, Cmnd. 9534, p. 15.

21. *Ibid.*, pp. 37–38. Sihanouk told Malcolm MacDonald (then British Commissioner General in Southeast Asia) in April, 1955, that he had considered the possibility of abdication for some time, "but that he only decided that the moment for the step had arrived when he was opposed in his wish to alter the constitution." Malcolm MacDonald, *Angkor* (New York: Frederick A. Praeger, 1959), p. 147.

22. Preschez, *op. cit.*, p. 60.

23. The sympathy of Communist writers for the Pracheachon is one indication of its affiliation. See Malcolm Salmon, *Focus on Indo-China* (Hanoi: Foreign Languages Publishing House, 1961), pp. 243–44.

24. *Fourth Interim Report of the International Commission for Supervision and Control in Cambodia*, Cmnd. 9671 (London: H.M.S.O., 1956), p. 11.

25. *Ibid.*, p. 17.

26. Preschez, *op. cit.*, p. 62.

27. *The Hindu*, September 14, 1955.

28. *Manila Daily Bulletin*, February 4, 1956.

29. *Ibid.*, February 7, 1956.

30. The aid agreement was made official in June, 1956. See "Joint Communique Issued by the Governments of China and Cambodia on the Question of Economic Aid to Cambodia, June 22, 1956," in G. V. Ambekar and V. D. Divekar (eds.), *Documents on China's Relations with South and South East Asia, 1949–1962* (Bombay: Allied Publishers Private, Ltd., 1964), pp. 314–15.

31. Herz, *op. cit.*, p. 128.

32. U. S. Department of State, *American Foreign Policy. Current Documents, 1956*. (Washington, D.C.: United States Government Printing Office, 1959), pp. 789–90.

4. THE PRACTICE OF NEUTRALITY

1. Quoted in Field, *op. cit.*, p. 173.

2. According to Herz (*op. cit.*, p. 127), the Chinese "let it be understood that if ever the Prince had trouble with the Viet-Minh, he need only appeal to Peking to have it stopped."

3. In Paris, Sihanouk gave a press conference in which he explained the domestic basis of his country's foreign policy. He pointed out that, after Geneva, the military elements of the Viet-Minh that had penetrated Cambodian territory had withdrawn, but they had left behind populations influenced strongly by their propaganda. To counter the danger of internal subversion, Sihanouk felt it necessary to demonstrate Cambodia's neutrality. He wished also to avoid Communist distrust, and therefore found it necessary to accept aid from both ideological camps. *Le Monde*, June 13, 1956.

4. *Bilan de l'oeuvre de Sangkum* (Phnom Penh), January, 1957, p. 44.

5. *Cambodian News* (Canberra), May, 1960, pp. 8–9.

6. A Thai source quoted frequently in Cambodia to justify this charge is Luang Vichitr Vadakarn, *Thailand's Case* (Bangkok: University of Moral and Political Science, 1941). The claims advanced in this work, however, would appear to relate to Laos and then only to two provinces. Cambodian concern most probably derives from the author's statement that half the territories which constituted French Indochina were taken from Thailand either by force or intrigue (p. 2).

7. David Wilson, "Bangkok's Dim View to the East," *Asian Survey*, June, 1961, p. 14.

8. The Cambodians were deterred equally by the difficulty of access to the temple from the bottom of the escarpment. See *Note on the Question of Prah Vihar* (Canberra, n.d.), p. 10.

9. The above account is taken from International Court of Justice, *Case Concerning the Temple of Prah Vihar (Cambodia and Thailand), Merits*, Judgment of June 15, 1962 (The Hague), pp. 31–32.

10. *Relations Between Thailand and Cambodia* (Bangkok: Ministry of Foreign Affairs, January, 1959), p. 7.

11. These fears were allegedly justified. *Ibid.*, pp. 5–6.

12. In September, 1965, following the revelation by the Prime Minister of Singapore of an incident involving the CIA, a subcommittee of the U.S. House of Representatives Foreign Affairs Committee began an investigation of the Agency. Among the catalog of incidents published at the time was

reference to a CIA attempt to foment a revolt against Sihanouk. See *The Times* (London), September 8, 1965.

13. During a rally in March, 1959, Sihanouk left no doubt about United States culpability: "Enfin nous devons mentionner les déclarations du second frère de Dap Chhuon, l'ex-deputé Slat Peau, révèlant qu'il était chargé de prendre des contacts reguliers avec une ambassade d'une grande nation seatiste. J'ai écrit au President Eisenhower pour demander l'intervention des Etats-Unis pour stopper 'ce patronage' illegal de nos voisins." *Principaux discours et allocutions de S.A.R. le Prince Norodom Sihanouk en 1959* (Phnom Penh, n.d.), pp. 24–25.

14. For a selection of Thai press comment, see *Petite anthologie de la presse thaie* (Phnom Penh: Ministry of Information, 1960).

15. See *Facts About the Relations Between Thailand and Cambodia* (Bangkok, October, 1961), p. 6. The Cambodian version of the speech in question does not contain any such remarks. See *Cambodian Commentary* (Phnom Penh: Ministry of Foreign Affairs, October–December, 1961), pp. 57–69.

16. *Facts About the Relations Between Thailand and Cambodia*, pp. 38–39.

17. The Cambodian Government made it clear that Sarit's insulting remarks were the cause of the diplomatic break. See *Livre blanc sur la rupture des relations entre le Cambodge et la Thailande le 23 Octobre 1961* (Phnom Penh: Ministry of Information, 1962). It also asserted that the Thai (and Vietnamese) attitude toward Cambodia was motivated by expansionism.

18. See *Aide memoire sur les relations khmero-thailandaises* (Phnom Penh: Ministry of Information, n.d.), pp. 36-38.

19. See, for example, *Réalités cambodgiennes*, November 10, 1961.

20. The decision of the Court was not without an ironic aspect. The Cambodians based their claim on a map said to be appended to the 1907 treaty between Thailand and France. However, the Court established that the map in question was unrelated to the 1907 treaty, but was the outcome of the treaty of 1904, which had provided for a mixed delimitation commission to establish the frontier along the Dangrek Range. The Commission did not perform its function for the part of the border along which the temple was situated. On the Commission's instructions, however, in 1907 a French surveyor made a map that placed the temple on the Thai side of the watershed but on the Cambodian side of the frontier. The Court ruled that, as Thailand had not objected to this error in the map until the 1958 negotiations, it had acquiesced in the demarcation. It therefore applied the principle of estoppel on the basis of fifty years of stable frontier.

21. *Réalités cambodgiennes*, August 2, 1958.

22. *Bangkok Post*, September 6, 1962. See also the general argument in Donald E. Nuechterlein, *Thailand and the Struggle for Southeast Asia* (Ithaca, N.Y.: Cornell University Press, 1965).

23. *Réalités cambodgiennes*, July 13, 1962.

24. *Réalités cambodgiennes*, July 6, 1962.

25. *Réalités cambodgiennes*, July 13, 1962.

26. Sihanouk claims that Mao told him, "If you wish to punish Ngo Dinh Diem, you can go right ahead and count absolutely on our aid and support. As for the Thais, we hope that you will soon come to an understanding with

them. They deserve careful handling, for at bottom they don't want an alliance with the Americans. Those who visit us here assure us that they were constrained and forced to submit to this alliance imposed by force and that they will try to get rid of it as soon as possible and adopt the same policy of neutrality as Cambodia." (*Réalités cambodgiennes*, July 6, 1962). It is of some significance that Chou En-lai sent his personal assurances to the Thai Prime Minister that China had no aggressive intent in exploding its first nuclear device. *Le Matin* (Phnom Penh), October 21, 1964.

27. *Réalités cambodgiennes*, July 13, 1962.
28. *Loc. cit.*
29. *Loc. cit.*
30. See Penn Nouth, *Memoire du Cambodge sur ses terres au Sud-Vietnam.* (Phnom Penh: Royal Palace, April, 1954).
31. *Further Documents Relating to the Discussion of Indochina at the Geneva Conference*, Cmnd. 9239, p. 6.
32. Permanent Mission of Cambodia to the United Nations, *Cochin-China Cambodian Territory* (New York, n.d.), p. 7.
33. See, for example, *Réalités cambodgiennes*, September 15 and 29, 1961.
34. See *Fifth Interim Report of the International Commission for Supervision and Control in Cambodia for the Period October 1, 1955 to December 31, 1956*, Cmnd. 253 (London: H.M.S.O., 1957), Appendix G, p. 35.
35. See, for example, *Réalités cambodgiennes*, July 20, 1962.
36. *Cambodian News*, May, 1960, p. 7.
37. See *Cambodge d'aujourd'hui* (Phnom Penh), March–April, 1960, p. 44.
38. See *Réalités cambodgiennes*, October 16, 1964.
39. *Seventh Interim Report of the International Commission for Supervision and Control in Cambodia, January 1, 1958–December 31, 1958*, Cmnd. 887 (London: H.M.S.O., 1959), pp. 2–8.
40. *Agence khmer de presse* (Phnom Penh), November 2, 1961.
41. *The Times* (London), September 8, 1961.
42. *The New York Times* correspondent Robert Trumbull, relates this episode in *The Scrutable East* (New York: David McKay Co., 1964), pp. 181–85.
43. In the speech made on his return from the Geneva Conference on Laos, in July, 1961. See *Cambodian News*, July, 1961, p. 2.
44. Reported in *The Times* (London), October 30, 1965.
45. See David Halberstam, *The Making of a Quagmire* (New York: Random House, 1965), p. 209.
46. Robert Trumbull reported that "United States Ambassador William C. Trimble has found it impossible to convince Sihanouk that Washington is unable to influence Thailand and South Viet-Nam to a more conciliatory tone in their relations with Cambodia." *The New York Times*, November 19, 1961.
47. See his comments about "the unjustifiable and unacceptable superiority of the white." *Kambuja* (Phnom Penh), April 15, 1965, p. 5.
48. At a cocktail party in Los Angeles, "A lady, large in heart and build," told Sihanouk: "Little man, we don't quite understand some of the things you've been saying, but we want you to know that we love you." Field, *op. cit.*, p. 246. This story is corroborated in Trumbull, *op. cit.*, pp. 188–89.
49. This premise would still appear to be operative. See Morton Halperin,

"China's Strategic Outlook," in Alastair Buchan (ed.), *China and the Peace of Asia* (New York: Frederick A. Praeger, 1965), p. 107.

50. Richard P. Stebbins, *The United States in World Affairs, 1956* (New York: Harper, 1957), p. 136.

51. See Field, *op. cit.*, pp. 203–5.

52. Sihanouk was certainly apprehensive where the overseas Chinese community was concerned. He rejected Mao's suggestion that Cambodia sign a dual citizenship treaty with China, as Indonesia had done. *Ibid.*, p. 201.

5. THE STYLE OF NEUTRALITY

1. Norodom Sihanouk, *Rapport au peuple khmer au terme de mission en Amérique et aux Nations Unies* (Phnom Penh: Ministry of Information, n.d.), p. 52.

2. For an example of the almost unparalleled flattery to which Sihanouk is subject in Cambodia, see *Kambuja*, October 15, 1965, p. 5.

3. See *Peking Review*, October 22, 1965.

4. *The Times* (London), October 19, 1965.

5. *The Guardian* (Manchester), October 18, 1965.

6. *Kambuja*, April 15, 1965.

7. October 25, 1961.

8. See Bernard K. Gordon, "Cambodia: Where Foreign Policy Counts," *Asian Survey*, September, 1965, p. 442.

9. In a speech of February 21, 1964, in the collection *Les Paroles de Samdech Preah N. Sihanouk*, January–March, 1964 (Phnom Penh: Ministry of Information, n.d.), p. 137.

10. Sihanouk, *Rapport au peuple khmer*, p. 3.

11. *Ibid.*, p. 8.

12. *Ibid.*, p. 82.

13. *Ibid.*, pp. 46-48.

14. *Cambodian Commentary* (Phnom Penh), October–December, 1961, p. 57.

15. *Kambuja*, July 15, 1965, p. 18.

16. *Cambodian News*, July, 1961, pp. 5–6.

6. DEVIATION FROM NONALIGNMENT?

1. Norodom Sihanouk, "Cambodia Neutral," p. 586.

2. *Ibid.*, p. 583.

3. *Loc. cit.*

4. See Bernard B. Fall, "South Viet-Nam's Internal Problems," *Pacific Affairs*, September, 1958.

5. According to Arthur J. Dommen, *Conflict in Laos: The Politics of Neutralization* (New York: Frederick A. Praeger, 1964), p. 115.

6. Referring to the dangers of what he described as "warm war," Sihanouk pointed out, "In fact this warm war can be carried on without risk to the great power sponsors, as it is conducted through the intermediary of small

nations in many parts of the world, particularly in the countries of Southeast Asia, having a common frontier with Cambodia." Reprinted in *Cambodian Commentary*, August, 1961, p. 6.

7. *Ibid.*, p. 11.
8. *Cambodian News,* January, 1961, pp. 17–18.
9. *Cambodian News,* March, 1961, pp. 10–11.
10. Field, *op. cit.*, p. 205.
11. See *Documents Relating to British Involvement,* Cmnd. 2834, pp. 156–58.
12. *Ibid.*, pp. 160–62.
13. Part of a broadcast statement by the Cambodian Government on April 13, 1961, pointed out: "If, however, the powers coming round to the idea of proposing as venue for the conference the town situated in the center of the neuralgic zone agreed that it should be held in Phnom Penh, the Royal Government is ready to face up to the obligations emanating from this choice." *Cambodian News*, April, 1961, p. 1.
14. See R. M. Smith, "Cambodia's Neutrality and the Laotian Crisis," *Asian Survey*, July, 1961.
15. He said in Tokyo, in October, 1961: "In truth it is now too late to hope for more than a leftward leaning neutrality. When on January 1, 1961, I called for a Conference on Laos, the relative position of the forces clashing in Laos made possible an agreement between the two blocs on neutralization. Five months later, when the West accepted the Geneva meeting, it was too late, for the Communists had won a complete military victory. From that time on the only neutralization of Laos, an improbably artificial neutralization, would be one granted by the Communists, probably based on compensatory concessions elsewhere in the world." *Cambodian Commentary*, October–December, 1961. p. 68.
16. See George Modelski, *International Conference on the Settlement of the Laotian Question, 1961–62* (Vancouver: Institute of Pacific Relations, 1963), p. 2.
17. See "Cambodia's Position Concerning the Laotian Problem," statement broadcast on April 13, 1961, published in *Cambodian News*, April, 1961, p. 1.
18. *Ibid.*, June, 1961, pp. 1–2.
19. Modelski, *International Conference*, p. 18.
20. *Cambodian News*, July, 1961, p. 2.
21. *Ibid.*, p. 11.
22. *Cambodian Commentary*, March, 1960, p. 7.
23. *Ibid.*, September, 1961, p. 11.
24. *Loc. cit.*
25. *Cambodian Commentary*, September, 1961, p. 11.
26. Sihanouk said, "We have too many memories in common which unite us. I cannot bring myself to lose an old enemy. I therefore prefer to allow the Pracheachon to continue to subsist."
27. *Ibid.*, pp. 20–21.
28. *Ibid.*, p. 21.
29. *Cambodian Commentary*, October–December, 1961, p. 13.
30. *Ibid.*, p. 67.
31. *Réalités cambodgiennes*, January 26, 1962.
32. *Cambodian Commentary*, October–December, 1961, p. 73.

7. THE DEMAND FOR A GUARANTEE

1. *Réalités cambodgiennes*, July 14, 1961.

2. The trend of events in both Laos and South Viet-Nam led *Réalités cambodgiennes* (March 16, 1962) to ask, "Combien de temps le pourrons-nous?"

3. As Modelski ("The International Conference on the Settlement of the Laotian Question," p. 32) points out: "Thus insult was added to injury (the general point of respecting Laos' wishes with regard to alliances having been conceded, there was no need to add the specific reference to SEATO); a defeat and another loss of nerve. No direct, tangible consequence flowed from this unnecessary concession, but its indirect political repercussions may well be incalculable. Most baffling of all is the apparent insensitivity to this of the American delegation in particular and its readiness to concede a public denial of the legitimacy of the American claim to exercise influence in this part of Southeast Asia."

4. *Ibid.*, p. 33.

5. After the crisis over the South Vietnamese claim that Cambodia was being used to provide asylum for the Viet-Cong, Sihanouk announced that the decisive factor in stopping an anti-Khmer maneuver was "the action of the Government of the Popular Republic of China which, in response to our appeal, loudly and clearly announced its intention of sending Chinese forces to assist Cambodia in the event of an attack by our neighbors." *Cambodian Commentary*, January–February, 1962, p. 9.

6. *Cambodian News*, October, 1962, pp. 1–2.

7. *Ibid.*, September, 1963, p. 8.

8. Abekar and Divekar, *op. cit.*, pp. 26–27.

9. *Cambodian Commentary*, January, 1960, p. 7.

10. It is significant that an official publication made reference to rebellious elements known as the "Viet-Cong," organized by and owing allegiance to the Vietnamese branch of the Communist movement; see *Cambodian Commentary*, September, 1961, p. 3.

11. For a detailed account of the Colombo Conference, see G. H. Jansen, *Afro-Asia and Non-Alignment* (London: Faber and Faber; New York: Frederick A. Praeger, 1966), pp. 330–51.

12. Around the time of the Colombo meeting, the government weekly *Réalités cambodgiennes* (December 21, 1962) pointed out, "Good relations with China are the keystone of our foreign policy."

13. *Survey of China Mainland Press*, No. 2920, February 15, 1963, p. 24.

14. *Jen-min Jih-pao* commented, "This sincere remark of Prince Sihanouk's encourages very much the Chinese government and people." *Survey of China Mainland Press*, No. 2976, May 10, 1963, p. 23.

15. *Survey of China Mainland Press*, No. 3034, August 7, 1963, pp. 22–26; No. 3036, August 9, 1963, pp. 32–33.

16. Norodom Sihanouk, "The Moscow Treaty and Us," *Neak Cheat Niyum* (Phnom Penh), September 1, 1963.

17. *Loc. cit.*

18. *Cambodian Commentary*, September, 1963, p. 4.

19. *Cambodian News*, January, 1963, p. 4.

20. *Cambodian News,* November, 1963.

21. *New York Herald Tribune,* June 1–2, 1963.

22. In its proclamation breaking off relations, the Cambodian Government stressed: "As a result, the Royal Government will in no way take any action which could aggravate the economic situation of the South Vietnamese people." The Cambodian port of Sihanoukville was still under development, and the Mekong River and the port of Saigon continued to provide a vital service.

23. He expressed his conviction in 1966 that "whereas Bao Dai had the good fortune to be exiled and nothing more, Ngo Dinh Diem was assassinated when he had ceased to give satisfaction." *Kambuja,* October 15, 1966, pp. 12–13.

24. *Réalités cambodgiennes,* July 5, 1962.

25. *Neak Cheat Niyum,* September 29, 1963.

26. *The Times* (London), November 23, 1963.

27. *The Times* (London), November 26, 1963.

28. *The Observer* (London), December 15, 1963.

29. *Loc. cit.*

30. *The New York Times,* January 7, 1964.

31. *Correspondence officielle sur le problème de la neutralité et des frontières du Cambodge* (Phnom Penh: Ministère des Affaires Etrangères, May, 1964), pp. 1–5.

32. *The Times* (London), January 28, 1964.

33. In a speech at Kep, February 16, 1964. See Sihanouk, *Les Paroles de Samdech Preah N. Sihanouk,* p. 111.

34. *Ibid.,* p. 134. Sihanouk was no doubt encouraged in this view by French recognition of Peking.

35. *Correspondence officielle, op. cit.,* p. 17.

36. *Ibid.,* p. 56. It should be pointed out that at the end of November, 1963, Sihanouk did concede that frontier differences could be the subject of separate negotiations. *The Observer* (London), December 1, 1963.

37. At the end of 1963, a South Vietnamese mission had visited Phnom Penh, and Huot Sambath had paid a return visit to Saigon. Hopes for progress in negotiations were upset, however, by General Khanh's coup on January 31, 1964.

38. Sihanouk, *Les Paroles de Samdech Preah N. Sihanouk,* pp. 294–95.

8. BLOCKED ROADS TO GENEVA

1. *Time,* April 3, 1964, p. 19.

2. *The Times* (London), March 25, 1964.

3. Dennis Bloodworth, in *The Observer* (London), April 4, 1964.

4. It should be noted that his request to Hanoi to state its position on the recognition of Cambodia's frontiers had brought a discouraging response. See *Les Paroles de S.P.N. Sihanouk, April–June, 1964* (Phnom Penh: Ministry of Information, 1964), p. 4.

5. *Réalités cambodgiennes,* July 4, 1964.

6. *Ibid.*

7. See Harold C. Hinton, *China's Relations with Burma and Viet-Nam* (Vancouver: Institute of Pacific Relations, 1958), pp. 1–24.

8. Sihanouk made it clear that his policy was in no way dictated by illusions. He pointed out: "Pour le moment, par exemple, l'intérêt des pays socialistes est de nous soutenir, de nous respecter. Notre intérêt a nous est d'accepter ce soutien et ce respect. Mais nous restons sans illusions a l'égard de quiconque. Entre governments, l'amitié n'est que la coincidence des intérêts." *Réalités cambodgiennes,* July 4, 1964.

9. *Le Monde,* July 7, 1964.

10. See *Le Matin,* October 17, 1964, which confirms that Sihanouk also arranged a meeting in Phnom Penh between N.L.F. representatives and exiled Vietnamese politicians.

11. *Agence khmer de presse,* reported by New China News Agency, August 10, 1964.

12. *Agence khmer de presse,* April 29, 1964, quoted by Jean-Pierre Simon in "Cambodia: Pursuit of Crisis," *Asian Survey,* January, 1965, p. 52.

13. It was alleged that Sihanouk's meeting in Paris with Vietnamese opposition leaders was preliminary to a meeting with representatives of the National Liberation Front. *Bangkok World,* October 4, 1964.

14. See his admission of this prospect in *Réalités cambodgiennes,* October 16, 1964.

15. An allegedly verbatim account of Sihanouk's conversations with Pham Van Dong in Peking is to be found in *Le Sangkum* (Phnom Penh), August, 1965, pp. 38–43.

16. See the Joint Sino-Cambodian Communiqué, in which the two parties agree that the problem of Indochina could be settled only in conformity with the Geneva Accords of 1954 and 1962 and by convening a conference of the countries concerned with these accords and by no other means. *Agence khmer de presse,* October 5, 1964.

17. See Alastair Buchan, *op. cit.,* p. 28.

18. *The Times* (London), November 10, 1964.

19. *Ibid.*

20. Dennis Bloodworth in *The Observer* (London), November 15, 1964.

21. AP and UPI Report, December 28, 1964.

22. See *Time,* January 8, 1965.

23. Statement over Radio Phnom Penh, December 22, 1963.

24. See *Discours de S.P. Norodom Sihanouk Upayuvareach, chef de l'état du Cambodge, a l'occasion de l'ouverture de la conference pléniere des peuples indochinoises* (Phnom Penh: Ministry of Information, February 25, 1965).

25. *The New York Times,* March 7, 1965.

26. Quoted in *Recent Diplomatic Exchanges Concerning the Proposal for an International Conference on the Neutrality and Territorial Integrity of Cambodia,* Cmnd. 2678 (London: H.M.S.O., 1965), p. 6.

27. For an account of the development of the institution of co-chairman, see *Documents Relating to British Involvement in the Indochina Conflict 1945–1965,* Cmnd. 2834 (London: H.M.S.O., 1965), p. 17 *passim.*

28. *Recent Diplomatic Exchanges,* Cmnd. 2678, pp. 4–5.

29. See *Recent Exchanges Concerning Attempts to Promote a Negotiated Settlement of the Conflict in Viet-Nam,* Cmnd. 2765 (London: H.M.S.O., 1965), pp. 43–48.

30. *The Times* (London), April 17, 1965.

31. *Recent Diplomatic Exchanges,* Cmnd. 2678, p. 11.
32. *Loc. cit.*
33. *Ibid.,* p. 14.
34. *Ibid.,* p. 15.
35. *Kambuja* (May 15, 1965, p. 3) commented: ". . . the American Government which had refused for years to allow a conference to be convened in Geneva for the purpose of providing us with a guarantee of our neutrality and territorial integrity, was suddenly struck with the idea that a conference of this nature on Cambodia might lead to the opening of discussions on Viet-Nam and thus give them the opening they were seeking to extricate themselves from the Vietnamese 'hornets nest.' The London Government, loyal executant of Washington's suggestions, lost no time in taking steps to bring about the convening of the proposed conference; a conference which was conceived with an almost complete disregard for our real interests, but appeared—on the contrary—to be another expedient devised by Anglo-Saxon diplomacy for the sole purpose of saving their stake in Asia."
36. *Recent Diplomatic Exchanges,* Cmnd. 2678, p. 17.
37. "Great Powers" in this context seems also to include North Viet-Nam. See *Kambuja,* June 15, 1965, p. 4.

9. HOW TO STAY NEUTRAL

1. *The Sunday Times* (London), May 16, 1965.
2. Harold Munthe-Kaas, "Interview with Prince Norodom Sihanouk," *Far Eastern Economic Review,* December 9, 1965, p. 457.
3. *Kambuja,* June 15, 1965, p. 21.
4. *Ibid.,* p. 25.
5. *The Times* (London), October 5, 1965.
6. *Kambuja,* January 15, 1966, p. 22.
7. *The New York Times,* October 12, 1965.
8. See *Peking Review,* October 22, 1965.
9. *Kambuja,* May 15, 1966, p. 14.
10. *The Guardian* (Manchester), November 10, 1965.
11. *Vietnam Courier* (Hanoi), February 17, 1966.
12. *The Guardian* (Manchester), December 22, 1965.
13. *Kambuja,* November 15, 1965, p. 10.
14. Reported in *The Times* (London), October 30, 1965.
15. *The New York Times,* October 14, 1965.
16. *Loc. cit.*
17. *The Guardian* (Manchester), November 10, 1965.
18. *The New York Times,* May 2, 1966. This charge was refuted by Harrison Salisbury, another correspondent of the same newspaper, June 10, 1966.
19. *Ibid.,* January 15, 1966, p. 13.
20. See *The Times* (London), January 4, 1966.
21. See *Vietnam Courier* (Hanoi), February 10, 1966.
22. For a published record of this meeting, see *Le Sangkum* (Phnom Penh), October, 1966, pp. 28–30.
23. *Réalités cambodgiennes,* July 8, 1966.

24. *Réalités cambodgiennes,* May 27, 1966.
25. *Kambuja,* December 15, 1965, p. 23.
26. *Réalités cambodgiennes,* October 29, 1965.

10. CONCLUSION

1. *Phnom Penh Presse,* June 24, 1966.
2. He made this view apparent during a conversation with the former chief minister of Sarawak. See *Kambuja,* April 1, 1966, p. 26.
3. See General Vo Nguyên Giap, "Once Again We Will Win," *Hoc Tap* (organ of the Viet-Nam Workers Party), January, 1966. Extracts from this article appeared in *Réalités cambodgiennes,* June 17, 1966.
4. *Réalités cambodgiennes,* May 20, 1966.
5. *Réalités cambodgiennes,* June 24, 1966.

Index

Acheson, Dean, 90
Agriculture, 4
Albania, 141
Alsop, Joseph, 180
Asian Games, 140–41
Auriol, Vincent, 43–44

Bandaranaike, Sirimavo (Mrs.), 139
Bandung Conference (1955), 62–63
Beck-Friis, Baron, 87–88
Boun Oum, Prince, 123
Brazzaville Declaration (1945), 28
Bundy, William P., 159
Butler, R. A., 146–48, 151

Cambodia: colonial period, 22–24; constitutional reform, 31–34; early history, 21–22; Japanese interlude, 24–26; *modus vivendi* with France of January 7, 1946, 28–29; neutrality, 61, 79, 80–84, 101, 187; relations with China, 138–42, 184–85, 190; and South Viet-Nam, 94–100; and Thailand, 84–93; and the United States, 101–4
Central Intelligence Agency, 88, 143–44
Cham-Malays, 10
Chantrea, 151–52
Chhoeun, Pach, 26–27, 31
Chieu, Hem, 26
Chinese minority, 10–12, 105
Chinese People's Republic, 60, 62–64, 163; attitude to conference on Cambodia (1965), 166–68; Cambodian diplomatic recognition of, 86, 98; declaration of friendship with Cambodia (1956), 74; relations with Cambodia, 104–5; Treaty of Friendship and Nonaggression with Cambodia (1960), 138; visits by Prince Sihanouk, 73–

74 (1956), 124 (1960), 140 (1963), 157–58 (1964), 175 (1965)
Chou En-lai, 12, 53–54, 62–64, 104, 163, 174–75
Cochinchina, 93–95
Colombo Conference (1962), 139–40

d'Argenlieu, Admiral, 28
Decoux, Governor-General, 25
De Gaulle, Charles, 25, 154, 157, 162
Democratic Party, 32–34, 69–70, 80
Diem, Ngo Dinh, 97, 143–44
Dien Bien Phu, 51
Dong, Pham Van, 53, 157–58
Dulles, John Foster, 44, 51–52, 57–58, 60, 77
Duong, Ang, 22–23

Economy, 6–9
Eden, Anthony, 51, 53–54
Education, 6
Eisenhower, Dwight D., 52, 58, 125

Fatherland Front of North Viet-Nam, 163
Foreign aid, 7–8, 60, 64, 74, 76–77, 156; rejection of United States, 144–45
France: attitudes to Cambodian independence, 27–49; colonial policy, 22–24; military and economic aid, 8, 156; visits by Sihanouk to, 43–44 (1953), 154–56 (1964)
Franco-Khmer Treaty (1949), 35–36

Geneva Conferences: on Indochina (1954), 52–55; on Laos (1961–62), 124–26, 133–34
Gordon, Bernard K., 113
Gordon Walker, Patrick, 165, 167
Grandière, Admiral de la, 23

207

Recto, Claro, 73
Religion, 5–6
Roosevelt, Franklin D., 28
✓ Royal Crusade for Independence, 43–49
Royal Khmer Socialist Youth, 15
Rusk, Dean, 149–50, 169

Sambath, Huot, 145, 149, 161
Sambaur, Yem, 34–35, 38, 41
San, Chea, 178, 184
Sangkum Reastre Niyum, 12, 14, 68–70, 109, 163
Sann, Sonn, 177
✓Sarit Thanarat, 85, 89–90
Sary, Sam, 53, 88, 100
✓ Sihanouk, Norodom, 12, 26–31, 35–37, 42–47, 49–50, 61–64; abdication, 66–68; conception of neutrality, 18, 71, 81–83, 120–21, 154–56; domestic conditioning and diplomatic style, 109–13; electoral success, 69–70; enthronement, 107–8; experience at United Nations (1960), 114–15; proposals for neutralization of Cambodia, 126, 130, 135; rejection of SEATO protection, 73; views on Laotian crisis, 122–26; on other neutrals, 116–19; on the war in Viet-Nam, 172–73
Sihanoukville, 96–97, 180
✓ Southeast Asia Treaty Organization, 57–59, 63, 75, 133
Souvanna Phong, 158
Souvanna Phouma, 121–22
✓ Soviet Union, 111; attitude to conference on Cambodia (1965), 164–70; attitude to enlargement of International Control Commission (1966), 183–84; visits by Sihanouk, 82 (1956), 124 (1960)
Stewart, Michael, 178
Stung Treng, 97–98, 181

Sukarno, 115, 118
Sulzberger, C. L., 181
Suon, Non, 131
Suramarit, Norodom, 12–13, 43, 68, 77

Test-ban treaty (1963), Sihanouk's response to, 141
✓Thailand, 25, 46, 74–76, 138, 191; relations with Cambodia, 84–93
Thailand Patriotic Front, 191
✓Thanh, Son Ngoc, 11, 16, 26–27, 39–41, 50, 65–66, 75, 84–85, 143
Thanom Kittikachorn, 90
Thuy, Xuan, 158
Tit, Khim, 27
Tonkin, Gulf of, incident, 157
Topping, Seymour, 179
Touré, Sékou, 118

✓United States of America, 51, 57–58, 64, 76, 88, 145; attitude to enlargement of International Control Commission (1966), 183; diplomatic break by Cambodia (1965), 169; negotiations over four-power conference (1964), 149–50; rejection of aid by Cambodia, 144–45; relations with Cambodia, 101–4; talks with Cambodia in New Delhi (1964), 161–62

✓Viet-Cong, 98–99, 179–83
Viet-Minh, 42, 45, 50, 60
✓Viet-Nam: North, 62–63, 96, 98, 135, 166, 182; relations with Cambodia, 93–100; South, 74–76, 142–43
Vietnamese minority, 10–11, 93, 95
Voeunsai, Sonn, 177

Wilson, Harold, 165, 169, 178

Youtevong, Prince, 32, 34